Netting the

SUN

A Personal Geography of the Oregon Desert

Netting the SUN

A Personal Geography of the Oregon Desert

by

MELVIN R. ADAMS

Melvin Adams

High Desert Conference 2001

WSU
PRESS

Washington State University Press
Pullman, Washington

WASHINGTON STATE UNIVERSITY

Washington State University Press
PO Box 645910
Pullman, Washington 99164-5910
Phone: 800-354-7360
Fax: 509-335-8568
E-mail: wsupress@wsu.edu
Web site: www.wsu.edu/wsupress

Library of Congress Cataloging-in-Publication Data

Adams, Melvin R., 1941-
    Netting the sun : a personal geography of the Oregon desert / by Melvin R. Adams.
      p. cm.
    Includes bibliographical references (p.).
    ISBN 0-87422-236-2 (pbk. : alk. paper)
      1. Oregon—Description and travel. 2. Oregon—History. 3. Oregon—Geography.
    4. Deserts—Oregon. 5. Natural history—Oregon. 6. Adams, Melvin R., 1941-
    I. Title.

F876 .A33 2001
979.5—dc21   00-068657

TABLE OF CONTENTS

Acknowledgments

I would like to thank the Lake County Historical Society and the Oregon Historical Society for permission to use a number of photographs associated with the history of Lake County. For their companionship on numerous trips into the Oregon outback and for sharing their knowledge of the Oregon desert, I thank Darrell Seven and Jean Sage, owners of the Summer Lake Inn. Mr. Jeff Fearnside, my editor at Washington State University Press, did the manuscript a tremendous service by his attentiveness to detail and thoughtful questions. For providing me four years of space and encouragement to prepare the manuscript and for enduring many rough desert roads, I thank my wife Onnie. I would also like to thank Terry Tempest Williams for her note of encouragement many years ago that provided the spark to begin this work.

In memory of
Roberta Bleakney

Going Home

*Can we ever love vastness
when we have known a
single tree as home?*

M Y JOURNEY in the Oregon desert began on October 20, 1941 when I was born in a hospital overlooking the small town of Lakeview, Oregon, in Lake County in the Goose Lake Valley. The hospital still exists, though it was converted to a private residence many years ago.

My mother had come to eastern Oregon from Arkansas in search of work and adventure and to escape the Great Depression. My father had come to the Goose Lake Valley from the Willamette Valley for mostly the same reasons, but he had a blind mother and a younger sister to support. He found work in the sawmills and wooden box factories at Willow Ranch on the shores of Goose Lake just across the California border.

Throughout her life, my mother worked out a genealogy in great detail. From her I found out about my Cherokee ancestors, Hudson of Hudson Bay fame, and the Mayo clinic. Somehow I was related to all of these things because of the names that appeared on her detailed family tree. In contrast, my father's ancestry remained a blank, impenetrable wall. He did not like to talk about his childhood, but I did know Ena, my blind grandmother who for a time lived in the house next door, and my aunt Marigold. Ena never kept a man or husband for more than a year or two, so I knew that my father had been raised by what seemed an endless succession of stepfathers, some rich, some poor, some abusive, and some generous. One of the stepfathers was named Adams. Near the end of my father's life I would discover in his files original fading documents signed by an M.V. Sweet. The documents indicated that my father had been left in Yakima, Washington, at the age of one with a nurse named Ena by his father, the mysterious Sweet. The documents stated that Millard, my father, was a sickly child who had been born in King County, Washington, and that if Sweet failed to reclaim his son after one year, Millard could be adopted by Ena. Despite my best efforts at genealogical research, Sweet remains a phantom. It is possible that he was taken by World War I, but I may never know for sure. Perhaps because of the succession of homes and stepfathers of his youth, my father never cared to venture far from the small house he built himself in Lakeview: a house finished just days before I was born. My parents were not well-educated, and they were scarred by the Depression in ways that I could never fully understand.

My youth in the high desert of Lake County revolved around hunting, camping, fishing, Boy Scouts, and the youth group of the local Mormon church. My parents had converted to Mormonism when I was about eight, and the church quickly became the focus of our social life. I grew up with a shotgun in one hand and a fly rod in the other. The round of outdoor activity was sometimes interrupted by the requirement of work on the church farm or an attempt to learn to dance with the Mormon girls at the church social hall. Looking back over the childhood of my own daughters, I realize that I was raised in an innocent, supportive, some would say naive, small town where drugs and crime were foreign concepts and where if you did something good, such as earning more scout merit badges, your name would be listed in the local newspaper.

Because of the influence of an English teacher named Roberta Bleakney and a math teacher named Laura Waterman, I was able to win a four-year college scholarship to Oregon State University from a fund left by a local pioneer doctor. Despite her limited formal education, my mother was an intelligent and cultured person, and she was determined that I would receive the education she lacked. My father was less supportive. He placed great stock in what he referred to as attendance at the school of "hard knocks." At college I gravitated to the natural sciences, returning home at holidays to hunt. During those years, I worked summers for the Forest Service as a logging road surveyor. This experience took me to the most remote reaches of Lake County in general and the Fremont National Forest in particular.

During my final summer in the Forest Service I took an interest in a Lakeview girl, also a student at Oregon State, and a few months later we married. Our first daughter was born in Burns, Oregon, where I held my first job as a science teacher. Following a year in North Dakota to obtain a master's degree in science, we moved to the San Francisco Bay Area, where our second daughter was born. During our decade in California, the Oregon desert continued to exert its influence. On summer breaks, we would take our daughters to camp in the Oregon desert, often in the same aspen groves where I camped as a road surveyor. I could often point out to my daughters that we were traveling on improved roads that I had surveyed.

After more than a decade in public education, my wife and I decided it was time to change locations and professions. We sold the California house and packed up our daughters so that I could return to college in Oregon to study environmental engineering. My new career quickly led to employment at the Hanford Nuclear Reservation in Washington state. At last, I was back in the desert, but in another state.

The Washington desert is much lower and dryer than the Oregon desert and, because of the Columbia river, much more populated, industrial, and wealthy from irrigated agriculture. Nevertheless, I became reacquainted with some of the desert icons of my youth—sagebrush, coyotes, tumbleweeds—though at Hanford, my efforts revolved around the practical matter of how to keep them out of radioactive waste disposal sites.

The Oregon desert is a day's drive on Highway 395 from our home in Washington state. The route winds through some of the most mountainous and uninhabited terrain left in the Pacific Northwest. Ironically, I have learned more about the history of this desert since I left because of vacation explorations I continue to make year after year. It is a sad irony of our educational process that we learn more about the flora, fauna, geology, and human history of our homes after we leave them than we learned while living in those places. Often the kings and queens of England get more attention in the curriculum than the rich history right outside our schoolhouse doors.

I know that I can never return to live in the Oregon desert: the winters are too cold, the inhabitants too insular, the road too far from my city-loving daughters. But, sometimes my wife or a daughter or my sister join me on the desert explorations of the homeland of my youth, though they do not seem to hear the siren songs of the desert or see its spirits and ghosts. Still, the desert muses are there, and they stake their claim on me. I know I will eventually have to plug my ears to them, but in the meantime they have prevailed upon me. The result is this book.

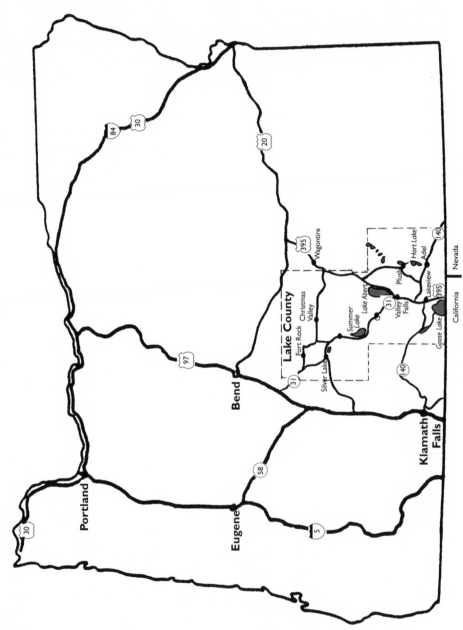

Map of Oregon, detailing Lake County.

Introduction

Do things loved
carry through, flicker
under glaciers, crystallize
in the sky, distill
as ash a little flower
perhaps near a desert spring?

MOST PEOPLE THINK of Oregon as a wet forest. Oregonians are often referred to as "webfeet" for, after all, the mascots of the two largest colleges are ducks and beavers.

But there is a dry side to Oregon constituting the half of the state that lies beyond the rain shadow of the Cascade Mountains. A large portion of the eastern half is a blank spot on a map, particularly the corner where the boundaries of Oregon, California, and Nevada meet. The counties that politically define the area are larger than several states and sparsely populated, at least with humans. This area is often called the high desert because the elevation is greater than a mile, with mountain ranges approaching ten thousand feet high. It can also be described as a cold desert, but more properly, it is geographically a steppe: a faulted, semiarid region of sage and grassland with few trees except for scattered junipers and pine forests isolated on the tops of north-south ranges overlooking a landscape of ancient lakes and alkali flats.

To the untrained eye, the region appears barren and relatively lifeless, a terrain to be endured while traveling from the gambling dens of Nevada to the wet side of Oregon. Recently in Adel, Oregon, I overheard a lady who had stopped for gas at the country store complain about what she had passed through on her way from Nevada to Portland. She did not see how anyone could live "out there." The store owner merely explained, "That's why we like it."

During the settlement of eastern Oregon by Europeans in the late nineteenth century, the region was called the "District of the Lakes" by the Army. General George Crook had established Fort Warner and was engaged in a campaign against the hostile natives. By that time the tribes, the shamans, and their cultures had largely been exterminated by disease, warfare, starvation, and displacement, yet the rock art of the shamans remains an enduring and permanent human feature on this landscape.

The District of the Lakes contains many lakes, but most are alkaline or dry. They were once large and deep and covered much of southeastern Oregon, but they have been drying for about ten thousand years, since the last ice age of the Pleistocene era. The "District" includes the political boundaries of Lake County, which contains 7,984 square miles and a human population of 7,186, a population density of about .9 persons per square mile. At the time of European contact, the native population was probably about 25 square miles per person.

I endeavored to write this collection of linked essays about the Oregon desert because of my childhood there, but also because it is a place of startling mystery, subdued danger, and beauty. It is a place to see nature raw, with most of our usual certainty taken from us. It is a place where the line between terror and beauty is thin and often crossed.

The original inhabitants of the Oregon desert created a symbolic art of place and engraved it on the rocks: illustrations of humans, animals, stars, and numinous beings so charged that there appears to be no difference between animate or inanimate, earth or sky, body or star, art or terrain. Such a place lays tenacious claims on the mind and heart and compels a return again and again.

The District of the Lakes is a historical metaphor for the settlement of the greater American West. All of the pivotal events of the West happened here, only less well-documented and on a less-noticed scale: range wars, Indian wars, gold rushes, booms and busts, and epic cattle drives. The region even boasted a ferry boat and mission architecture, but on a much smaller scale than San Francisco.

I also endeavor to portray the region because it is still relatively undisturbed and visible. There are still unnamed spaces on a map and geographic features without a name. There are unresolved tensions between pagan animism on the one hand and an extractive civilization on the other. It is not clear how the story will end. By attempting to understand this place, I was able to reconstruct the geography of my own beginnings and my own nature and to reveal, because of this place, the hidden parts of my own nature.

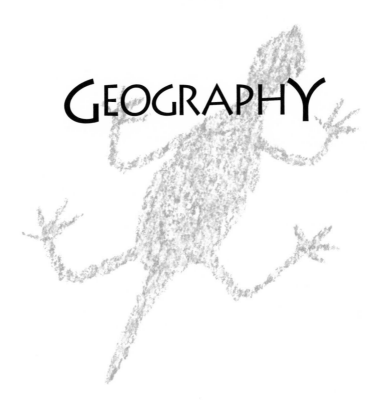

PART ONE

GEOGRAPHY

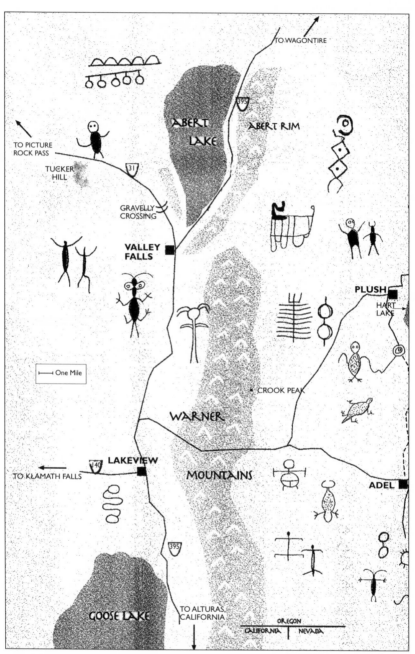

Section of map of south-central Lake County, including replications of various petroglyphs from the area. *(Map designed by Carrie Adams)*

ONE

The High Desert

Here on this wind field,
in the dry and salty sun,
piles of animal skulls,
distillations, flirtations and toys
of bones
tossed on rock shelves
barren as the moon,
forgotten in cabinets
of time and night.

I WENT TO THE DESERT to become reacquainted with childhood and its primitive thoughts and dreams, to rediscover basic truths, to return to the territory where I was born and raised. Evidence is exposed in the desert: bones of animals caught in a blizzard; burned sage skeletons, the result of dry, electrical storms; scoured gullies that spew torrents when it occasionally rains. The desert is anchored in extremes: either too much water or not enough; nighttime freezes and mid-day heat; gentle, mild breezes and then suddenly a cold burst of snowy wind. Even the colors of the desert are extreme: subtle and flat at mid-day but exploding to vivid reds, oranges, purples at sunrise or sunset. The desert at times saturates with color; the rocks and grass exude it; the rims glow as if ignited by an invisible neon gas in the hard rock pores.

I went to the desert to find the simple and plain in the world and in myself: to find the basic elements of salt, fire, rain, sun, grass, and sage; to find their scents and meanings; to find the primal elements of the desert and myself. The desert cannot be survived without preparation and attention. It is honest in its intention. There is no false sense of security there as one might find in more vegetated regions.

The skeleton of time is revealed in the desert; no layers of sod or humus cover the foundation of the earth. The Pleistocene is stripped bare for the eye to see all the way to the beginning of human habitation and before. Ancient bones are as likely to be exposed by wind one day as the next. There is nothing to absorb or moderate the forces that polish, grind, and tear at the earth's skin and at our own mental certainty. All is revealed here given enough time. Human history yields a cow or sheep skeleton here, a rusted horseshoe there, a fading wagon wheel or hay rake covered in dust and sand, an abandoned ranch from what was once an empire. The lake shores from the last ice age are as visible today as they were ten thousand years ago. The earth is stripped down to its volcanic foundation, like an ancient text in an old room covered with dust.

The sky is immediate in the high desert, the storms and clouds close to the ground. The day sky is more solid blue and the night sky more black. There are no disturbing lights or sounds or mists or fogs. The moon and stars spring directly from notches in rim rock. The horizon daily gives birth to constellations and planets. There is no barrier or filter between earth and sky; the constellations are more populated with stars, and their light is undiluted.

I went to the desert to be astonished by spring and wildflowers that grow in rock gardens where no soil or water appears to collect, astonished by bare rock covered with lichens in saturated reds, oranges, and yellows. How is it possible to live like this—in the freezing wind one day and a torrid gale the next? I became amazed by galloping antelope and drumming sage grouse and by the simplicity of life and its durability.

I went to the desert to be tested; to exorcise pride and self-concern; to dissolve layers of human presumption; to recover the elemental where there is no difference between man, animal, wind, rock, sun, or grass; to find the intersection of the animate and inanimate. In the desert I found a heartbeat: rhythms of grass, flutterings of aspen, murmurs of ancient wind. I am happy there.

In the desert are pools that taste of the salt of existence, briny lake waters and hot springs close to the earth's molten heart. In the desert is the territory before man where there is not a name on every lake or trail, and sometimes there is no map at all.

There emanates a certain tragic sense in the desert, no assurance there of success or even life. There are voices and signs in the desert: some carved by time and wind, some by the shamans, the ancient astronomers. The original inhabitants knew the desert in all of its manifestations. They were conscious of their own collective soul but did not impose it on the outside world around them; they found entities in rocks, stars, and animals. They were conscious of the force of life all around them in everything, and they sought to draw the power into themselves. There are stories in the desert, on the rocks and in the alkaline ground. Some of the stories are theirs, and some of the stories are mine.

TWO

Long Lake

Voices fall
like soft desert rain
like cranes
calling in the night,
unseen, lost,
but palpable,
present but
mysteriously
folded in distance.

WE JOSTLED ALONG rough roads all day. Gullies and rocks impeded progress at times to a crawl. It was late, and we were lost. Since we were without camping gear, it was important to get back to a decent road before dark, although the long, clear days of September would help. My petroglyph-hunting friend Darrell and I tried to decipher our location from the topographic maps. Unconcerned, my wife and sister were happy with the day of seeing deer, antelope, mountain sheep, mountain bluebirds, sage grouse, sheepherders' cabins, abandoned ranch houses, and vast stretches of uninhabited sage and bunch grass. We were in the middle of a part of southeastern Oregon visited by few except the infrequent hunter, rancher, or wildlife biologist from the Hart Mountain Antelope Refuge, a region called by some the Serengeti of North America.

We were trying to find Long Lake, the alleged location of a petroglyph site. I finally convinced Darrell to continue straight ahead—a risky move if the road became impassable and caused us to backtrack and waste more daylight. About a half-hour later, though, I saw it. The low basalt rim stretched for over two miles along a dry lake bed. Near the lake we were able at last to pinpoint our position on the map using a section corner and plot a path back to the main road. Only about two hours could be devoted to exploration before we would have to leave. Determined to make the most of the time, I stuffed my pockets with film. I knew it would be a full year before the climate, weather, and schedules would allow me to return.

The rim near the dry lake had a north-south orientation and was about twenty-five to thirty feet high. According to the topographic map, the lake bed lay 6,059 feet above sea level. As I walked, the meaning of Eliade's word "heirophany," the manifestation of the sacred in the ordinary, became evident. Even a marvelous visit to the Guggenheim museum in New York with my daughter some years earlier had not prepared me for this rim rock. There were petroglyphs on every smooth basalt rock face, petroglyphs stacked above each other clear to the top of the rim, petroglyphs on the tops of boulders near the rim. Later I would find that petroglyphs extended to below the lake sediment on the rim and that an archaeologist had dated them at sixty-six hundred years before present because they were covered with ash from the eruption of Mount Mazama.

There were also rock shelters and small caves still black with the soot of countless fires, rock walls used as hunting blinds near the lake, and cairns and stone circles on top of the rim. A few rare painted pictogram figures were also evident. The art depicted rainbows, mythical horned creatures, winged creatures, human forms in the posture of ascent, horned animals, zigzags and geometric arrangements of countless dots, cup-like engravings, ladder figures, centipedes, snakes and lizards, hunters with atlatls and bows, crescent moons, suns, constellations, stars, historical geographies, and other signs and symbols. I began to feel a mysterious attraction to the place as if it were a cathedral, a gallery of sacred art, a primitive testament, a tragedy, a gift, a mystery. I felt as if some cataclysm could happen at any time, that some terrible event or events had happened to sanctify the place. It seemed hallowed ground. Mostly I felt alone and inconsequential, as if gods had set loose forces far beyond the ability of humankind to control but that the artists here had somehow seen and recorded. Two hours later we were only halfway down the rim. The petroglyphs continued. I took over two hundred pictures.

This trip would mark the beginning of a personal journey to understand the petroglyphs there and at the many other sites we would later visit nearby. I return every summer to Long Lake; each visit uncovers new mysteries; each trip is an encounter with raw beauty. Something always happens to remind me of human fragility: high winds, violent thunderstorms, experiences with animals. All these events seem more intense in the high, clear air. The ancient petroglyphs only add to the mystery. Perhaps it is because we are so exposed in such an open and elemental place that it is so attractive and intriguing to the imagination.

THREE

Metaphors

*Met•a•phor n.—something used, or regarded
as being used, to represent something else;
emblem, symbol.*
—Webster's Dictionary

WHAT IS THE METAPHOR for the experience of the Oregon desert? What musical notation, mathematical formula, word, symbol, or artifact can represent it and take up residence in the human mind, a mind full of metaphors? Was there a Vivaldi of the desert, this desert, creating seasons from sounds intelligible in any language? Was there a desert god like the God of Genesis commanding a world into existence, a word creating a world? Was there an Einstein of the desert imagining the universe while riding a beam of light, creating star formulae, cosmic speed limits from a perfect mathematical metaphor in two variables? Was there a Newton of the desert watching objects fall, watching the moon fall around the earth in mathematical precision? Was there a Picasso of the desert painting a *Guernica*: a metaphor of horror and inhumanity? Yet, in Picasso's painting a bird's beak reaches up to its parents' food and a flower blooms near a severed arm, metaphors of ultimate redemption.

The Australian aboriginals create haunting, vivid patterns of color: map metaphors for the song lines of creation where ancestors sang the land into existence, a mountain for a note here, a hymn for a valley there. Their art is a map, the map becomes a path, the path becomes a song, the song becomes a land, and the land becomes a history. Stop singing and the land dies; history dies also, such are they linked.

Is there a metaphor for the god of this desert world: a metaphor equal to Melville's great white whale of a god at loose on the seas of this world? Can a land or place fully exist until an artist creates it in words and sounds and symbols? Is there a cartographer of the desert creating with line and symbol the springs and mountains and dry lakes until they stand up and live on flat paper?

The Ayllu people of the Andes find in their home a metaphor of a human body, according to Joseph Bastien, who has studied their mythology. The highlands of Apacheta are the head, and the lowlands of Ninokorin are the toes. The mountain of the Ayllu is literally a body with lakes for eyes and rivers for arms and legs. The mountain has a heart and a mouth, and in ritual the Ayllu feed the mountain to maintain the balance of the world. Perhaps a body metaphor could be constructed for the Oregon desert, complete with graben navels, horst sinews, basalt skin, aspen hair, lake mouths, and springs for eyes with tears.

On the rock rim above Long Lake stands a stone circle twenty-four feet in diameter and about four feet high. Sighting stones and portals in the rock wall align with Hart Mountain to the north and Little Juniper Mountain to the south. About one hundred feet north of the circle is a stone animal head, about waist high, poised over a sighting stone which also aligns with the faulted notch in Hart Mountain. The animal head has been inscribed with eyes and a mouth. When viewed from the center of the circle, some of the perimeter stones and portals in the circle wall appear to point to stars and constellations, probably at the solstice or equinox. Is it a stone metaphor—a map frozen in time, encrusted with red lichens? Is it a direction finder—an alignment of mind with land and star, a stellar and terrestrial geography, one merging into another?

Within the circle on the north side, a flat rock facing inward to the circle bears a petroglyph. It is the stick figure of a shaman with a headdress of rays bursting from the head. Is the body Long Lake? Is the head an unnamed lake to the north? Do the figures, circles, and dots represent nearby lakes: Wildlife lakes, unnamed lakes, Moon Lake, Weed Lake? The pattern of lakes seems to match the modern topographic metaphor of the surveyors, but the ancient "map" is more. The metaphor in stone may be a model of their land and a model of the native mind. But perhaps their land and their mind and their body were all the same. The land must have inhabited them as surely as their blood, engraved in their minds like a neural network, and they engraved it on stone. In a remote desert, the wind howls over a barren stone circle encrusted with time: a picture of the land, the metaphor of the mind of the desert rendered in stone.

FOUR

The Geography of Names

The poet is the Namer or Language-Maker,
naming things sometimes for their appearance,
sometimes after their essence,
and giving to every one its own name
and not another's.
—Ralph Waldo Emerson

THINGS DO NOT REALLY EXIST in the human world until they are named. How else to explain the compulsion to name every feature of a landscape, every plant, animal, and even insect? It is unheard of for a person not to have one or more names given at birth or soon after. The need to name and the power associated with naming goes to the root of our religious experience. In the Old Testament, the earth and everything on it, including humans, were ordered into existence by the commands of God. For the aboriginals in Australia, the land did not exist until their ancestors sang it into existence in the dream time. The aboriginals recreate and maintain existence by walking, naming, and singing as did their ancestors.

According to the Achomawi tribe, the Oregon desert was formed by silver fox singing to a clump of sod, the foundation of the created world.

Emerson thought that the poets made all the words, that language was the archive of history, and that poetry is a fossil language. Even though the origin of most words is forgotten, each word was a stroke of genius according to him. Certainly no place seems entirely to exist without its literature and poet: the sea had Melville, the sand hills of Nebraska had Cather, Africa had Hemingway, Big Sur had Jeffers, and Monterey and the Salinas Valley had Steinbeck. What would the Sierras be without Muir?

Carved aspen tree near Colvin Lake, due east of Abert Rim. *(Melvin Adams)*

The Oregon desert also had poets—the shamans, masters of a non-alphabetical but symbolic graphic language. They defined the land in terms of animal spirits, flights of the soul, constellations, moon and sun, sky nets, ascensions, and dreams. Their literature stretches thousands of years across a boundary of time and culture. In this they belie the name "primitive" we often give to them because the European mind has yet to record the visceral impact of the mysterious and haunting Oregon desert.

The explorers, sheepherders, and ranchers named the geographic features important to them by marking initials and brands on aspen trees and a few rocks, but their efforts do not compare to the thousands of rocks marked by the artwork of the shamans either in quantity or in the invocation of the nature of the land. They were in a hurry to make money and move on rather than stay in a place and fix on it an artist's impression of the human experience with the land. There is an exception, however. At Jack Lake can be found a petroglyph made with a steel tool, probably the work of a European settler. The petroglyph depicts a lake with a large fish and a turtle; sunbursts and virga rain down from clouds, antlered animals graze, and conical dwellings appear on the shore. The depiction is a human expression, however crude, of love for a place. The choice of the turtle by a European is intriguing because turtle plays in the creation story of several tribes. It was the animal that brought mud from the bottom of the world sea to provide a place for earth mother to stand on and complete creation.

In the Oregon desert, Lake County alone has five million acres and about two thousand named geographic features—about one named feature for every twenty-five hundred acres. Such an open and sparsely named land is like a blank tablet on which the stuff of imagination and dreams can be sketched. What did the European do in naming the features of the Oregon desert? To find out, it is necessary to examine the place name index of the Lake County map. Because of the economic importance of water in a semi-arid land, the most-named features relate to water: springs, lakes, reservoirs, streams, creeks, and even wells. Of these, springs are the most commonly named feature. Of the more than two hundred springs named in Lake County, eighty-one were given human surnames. Objects provided names for the next most common group. Only one spring was named for a state—ironically, Arkansas—perhaps in honor of the influx of loggers and miners from Arkansas and Oklahoma during the dust bowl and Great Depression. Even though birds and animals have lived in the area since the beginning of time, only fifteen springs are named for animals and three for birds; animal parts, such as "antler," claim nine names; plants and tree names were used eighteen times. One spring was named for a sound, "roaring." Five springs were named for adversity such as "horror" and "dismal." A few springs were named for colors, including "blonde." One spring sports the name of the letter "T"—probably the initial of the namer of the spring. As for the natives who lived for thousands of years in the area, only one spring has a clearly Indian name, but six springs were unimaginatively named "Indian" and one was named Dead Indian Spring.

Next after bodies of water, the most commonly named features in Lake County are buttes. Being volcanic country, there are many buttes, but only sixty-three of them have names. Again, human surnames dominate; birds, Indians, plants, and animals receive little recognition.

Clearly, the power of naming goes to the invading culture with a written—as contrasted to purely oral—language; or could it be that the petroglyphs are really the names of things, names so beautiful and complex that we simply cannot understand?

FIVE

Blank Spots on a Map

I would rather wake up in the middle of
nowhere than in any city on earth.
—Steve McQueen

FOR THE FIRST NINETY-NINE HUNDRED YEARS of habitation, the landscape of the Oregon desert was populated with immaterial souls, beings, and spirits, all of which inhabited the minds of the natives. The landscape abounded with deer, antelope, big horn sheep; the drying lakes and remnant wetlands teemed with such great clouds of ducks, geese, and birds that we can scarcely imagine the numbers. The streams that drained into the landlocked lakes overflowed with native trout, tui chubs, and suckers. The native people sought to take into themselves the power of the spirits found in animals, plants, trees, and rocks. The hunters and gatherers lived for thousands of years in this abundance while their shamans used the landscape as an astronomical flying field to launch their trance-like flights of the soul.

Europeans arrived on this land in 1832, when John Work explored the area for the Hudson's Bay Company, looking for the wealth to be found in beaver pelts. John Fremont and Kit Carson followed in 1843 to locate the imagined Buena Ventura River for the government. The mythic river was thought to provide an easy waterway access to the Pacific which would enable the rapid expansion of the United States. Later, Capt. William Horace Warner would also be sent to search for a railroad pass to the same river and lose his life. The dream of western expansion was written on the blank map of the high desert. By the time these and other explorers reached the region, the native tribes had already been reduced to a mere fraction of their original populations due to European diseases that preceded the actual arrival of the white man.

Next came the dream of the pioneers for land and gold. Emigrant trains probably passed Goose Lake as early as 1847. In his journal of 1853, Welborn Beeson describes his first encounter with Goose Lake from the Applegate trail. "Then on the summit we can see over a vast valley below us, heavy timber on each side and Goose Lake glistening through the trees. There are plums and all kinds of wild berries on the mountains. Goose Lake is a large body of water full of water fowl of every description." A decade earlier a group led by Col. Joseph Chiles described Goose Lake's "beautiful, romantic sheets of water." M.T. Walters, an early settler in the valley, described the current town site of Lakeview as "a beautiful meadow all covered with water where wild birds and animals looked at me in shy surprise."

For many emigrants, the arrival at Goose Lake forced a choice: continue to the Rouge River or Willamette Valley in search of an agricultural paradise or bear south to the gold fields of California. Later, near the beginning of the twentieth century, a gold rush small in comparison to California's would occur in the very Warner Mountains the emigrants passed through. With the settlers came General Crook, Fort Warner, and the first military roads to help protect the settlers and emigrants. It was only a matter of time before the last bands of hostiles would be killed, starved, or placed on reservations.

The next dream to be sketched in a blank spot on the map involved cattle. Pete French drove herds from California to the open range lands near Steens Mountain and the Shirk family built an empire further to the south with stock driven from Texas. It was only a matter of time before empires would collide in gunshot and bloodshed. Range conflicts heightened with the arrival of sheep and the Irish and Basque who tended them. At shearing time, the streets of Lakeview used to be filled with wool wagons bound for the markets of San Francisco, but by the 1930s the range was so depleted that the government had to regulate grazing under the Taylor Grazing Act. The sheep population declined to a few thousand and the remaining cattle spreads were bought by large corporations or remained in the possession of families who struggled to preserve the traditional, independent, ranching lifestyle in the face of governmental intervention and control over most of the land.

By 1936 the once-large herds of pronghorn antelope were in such danger of disappearing altogether that President Franklin Roosevelt was prevailed upon to devote a 250,000-acre refuge at Hart Mountain for their protection. Even then the cattle culture was so strong that grazing continued on the refuge until just a few years ago when a court order suspended the practice. In the meantime, the once-abundant bighorn sheep had entirely disappeared on Hart Mountain except as pictures on petroglyphs; only in recent years have small numbers been reestablished on Hart Mountain and Abert Rim.

In north Lake County, the homestead acts brought dreams of land ownership and families from the east who did not understand the climate or conditions of the high desert. Many small towns were created, and some opened post offices, schools, and newspapers, but within a few years most had starved out, leaving abandoned dwellings, abandoned dreams, and blowing sand on the disturbed land. Today dune fields shift silently near the homesteads: a reminder and a result of failure.

During the 1930s and 1940s still a different dream began to materialize on the rich wetlands and peat bottoms of the Warner Valley. The Kittredge family began using large equipment to drain and control the water flowing into the Warner Valley from the Warner Mountains. They became rich from cattle and grain, but only at the expense of the migratory birds, the land, and themselves: a modern-day lesson in hubris, which is well documented in the writings of their son, William.

In the late 1930s and early 1940s, necessity and another wave of new hope arrived to fill the blank spots on the map. From Arkansas and Oklahoma came people eager to escape the Great Depression and the dust bowl, including my own mother. Men found work as loggers or in the sawmills, and women as cooks or nannies or seamstresses. A few women also worked in the wooden box factories that turned out fruit boxes for the orchards of California. World War II accelerated the reduction of the ponderosa pine groves in the mountain plateaus surrounding the high desert. For a short time, the semi-arid forests of eastern Oregon turned out more lumber than the much more humid and fast-growing forests west of the Cascade Range. It could not last. Today only a single mill struggles on, cutting small timber in the once-grand ponderosa pine groves of Lake County.

Other blank spots on the map have been subject to military exploitation. During World War II, the uninhabited high desert was used as a gunnery range for navy pilots stationed at a hastily constructed airfield in Lakeview. Nearby in Klamath County, Japanese Americans were placed in tar shack prisons at Tule Lake while many of their sons fought for America in Europe. Remains of their temporary quarters still stand at New Pine Creek and near Goose Lake, subsequently used by ranchers as storage sheds. During the cold war, uranium was mined from aspen groves west of Lakeview. Those mines have remained a sore on the land, still waiting for federal tax dollars to help clean up the mess promoted by nuclear armament.

The clouds of birds my father took me to see in Warner Valley are no more; only remnants remain of the Pacific Flyway. The swarms of large, fat native trout in Deep Creek are no longer present to tantalize a young boy with a willow fly pole. Stories of being able to stand in one place in Deep Creek and catch as many trout as you wanted with a bucket can no longer be imagined. The roll call of endangered, threatened, and rare plants and animals in the high desert grows: Goose Lake sucker, Pit sculpin, Catlow tui chub, Summer Basin tui chub, Goose Lake tui chub, Sheldon tui chub, Foskett Spring speckled dace, Warner Basin tui chub, California roach, Pit-Klamath brook lamprey, Goose Lake lamprey, Goose Lake redband trout, Warner Valley redband trout, vagrant pebblesnail, Abellan hydropsyche caddisfly, XL springsnail, gold-hunter's hairstreak butterfly, thick-antennaed current bug, Oregon pearly mussel, Stretch's satyr butterfly, Warner Valley titmouse, Warner Valley Bewick's wren, black-throated sparrow, thick-stemmed wild cabbage, green-tinged paintbrush, yellow lady's-slipper, Great Basin dowingia, cupped dowingia, Crosby's buckwheat, Cusick's buckwheat, prostrate buckwheat, Boggs Lake hedgehyssop, discoid goldenweed, Cooper's goldflower, grimy ivesia, Shelly's ivesia, Shockley's ivesia, least rush, California lophotocarpus, smooth malacothrix, nodding melic, broad-toothed monkeyflower, Lemmon's false-caraway, playa phacelia, desert allocarya, Oregon semaphore grass, verrucose sea-purslane, Malheur stylocline, long-flowered snowberry, and short-podded thelypody.

It is possible to imagine the District of the Lakes as a boneyard of failed dreams, an open-sky museum of abandoned artifacts. Ample evidence is provided by abandoned corrals, rusting machinery, bones and skeletons of cattle and sheep caught in blizzards, buried toxic wastes, open-pit uranium and gold mines, ghost towns, unused military ammunition bunkers, wigwam burners and old sawmill machinery, decaying livery stables, logged-over stump fields, falling shearing sheds, ill-maintained roads, blowing sand, and overgrazed stream banks. The history of dependence on extraction having failed them in less than one hundred years, and being unable to imagine the opportunities in trade and technology carrying most of Oregon to prosperity, local leaders now seek to host state prisons to save a faltering economy. Some residents fear that the area will become a repository of toxic cultural refuse as real as the toxic wastes buried at Alkali

Lake. Still others cling to the dream of extractive wealth, unable to see how little is left to extract. The tension between exploitation and restoration runs across the high desert as clear as a fault line.

Many remaining residents in the high desert hold a fiercely independent attitude toward government intervention, but seem blind to the irony that from the earliest days settlers in the area have depended on the government for roads, for protection from Indians, for grazing and timber harvesting regulation, and for land restoration. Most of the land is owned by the government (ranchers rely on low-cost grazing leases on that land) and the government is the largest employer. The cattle empire of Pete French has become a federal wildlife refuge, and the decaying remains of the Shirk ranch house sit on land sold to the U.S. government.

Will those prevail who want to extract what remains from the land and allow it to become a repository for what no one else wants? There is hope for a different end in recent, progressive challenges to the longheld paradigm of extraction. Some cattle production is occurring that is consistent with preserving habitat for wildlife. The Nature Conservancy bought and is restoring the Sycan Marsh in cooperation with ranchers. The Conservancy also bought a ranch in the Warner Valley, leased an area to protect the semaphore grass, and has worked with governmental and private groups to restore nineteen thousand acres of wetlands in the Warner Valley. A consortium of conservation groups has proposed the establishment of forty-seven wilderness areas, a new wildlife refuge at Lake Abert, fifty-four wild and scenic rivers, three national monuments, and a Steens Mountain National Park—all in the high desert of Oregon. It's a large dream for a large land.

As I look back on the blank spots on the map of my youth, I stand off and view it with love as might one lost and gone for a long time. Despite all of the wreckage on it, it still lays claim to my imagination. Its barren soul still demands attention, and it is still illuminated with an indescribable crystalline light. It is permeated with mystery, and I know it will claim my last thoughts.

PART TWO

ORIGINS

AND

ELEMENTS

SIX

Horst, Graben, and Asteroid

Beneath this solidified fire,
imprints of leaf and wing
remember the dirty rain,
the leaden sky of the beginning.

A CCORDING TO ONE geologic theory I happen to like, the high desert originated about seventeen million years ago when an asteroid several miles across appeared in the sky over what is now the Oregon desert. As the stone entered the atmosphere, the air was heated to thousands of degrees. Shock waves of hot air blasted the terrain, killing all living things in its path. When the space rock slammed into the earth, earthquakes of biblical proportions occurred. The impact formed a crater perhaps one hundred miles in diameter, and the friction and energy of momentum melted the asteroid and layers of earth, forming a huge lava lake. As the lava began to flow away and the lake dissipated, new lava welled up from the earth's mantle, which had been breached by the impact. When the lava cooled some 1.5 million years later, most of southeastern Oregon was blanketed with basalt thousands of feet thick and covering over six thousand square miles. I like this theory because I believe the shamans who carved on the basalt rocks of the desert would have liked it. They lived in the sky, watching for signs of impending cataclysm.

After the asteroid but still ten million years before present, the rocks of southeastern Oregon were placed under tension as if a giant were pulling taffy. The tension broke up the basalt along north-south parallel fault lines extending hundreds of miles. Mountain-sized blocks of rock moved up or down between the fault lines: the upward thrust blocks formed

View of Hart Mountain looking east from Warner Valley. *(Melvin Adams)*

mountains or horsts; the downward thrust blocks formed basins called grabens. The horsts are clearly seen today, including Abert Rim, with a sheer rim two thousand feet high, and Hart Mountain, with a rim three thousand feet high. The grabens filled eventually with sediment and water and salt. About ten thousand years ago during the Pleistocene ice age, the graben lakes were hundreds of feet deep, and camels, elephants, giant beaver, horses, bison, large cats, and even flamingos lived near the lake shores. To this day the fault lines are conduits bringing hot, molten rock near the surface to create the many hot springs, geysers, and earthquake swarms in the desert.

It was during the last ice age that large U-shaped canyons were gouged by glaciers in the horst called Steens Mountain. Even some of the intrusive volcanic cones at the western edge of the basin and range, such as Gearhart Mountain, were glaciated; Dairy Creek today drains from a glacial bowl or cirque in the side of Gearhart. Further west, the younger explosive volcanoes of the Cascade Range erupted, including Mount Mazama, which sixty-six hundred years ago spewed ash over much of the Pacific Northwest, leaving a crater now called Crater Lake.

The volcanic cones of the Cascades created a rain shadow which blocks and drains the moisture from Pacific storms before they reach the desert to the east. It was only a matter of time after the Cascades formed that eastern Oregon would evolve into a sage-and-grass, semi-arid desert. Today, old shorelines, dry salt flats, salt lakes, mud cracks, dust storms, ephemeral streams and playa lakes, fossil bones, and dry earth testify to the drying of the climate after the glacial period.

Luckily for humankind, an asteroid has not revisited the area for the last seventeen million years, but a few small reminders of our vulnerability descend upon on us from time to time. In 1938, deer hunters near Goose Lake found a meteorite weighing over a ton; it remains the largest meteorite in the Smithsonian Institution. In 1994, a fireball entered the sky over eastern Oregon, changing in color from blue-white to green to yellow to red before exploding into pieces. Sonic booms were heard over one hundred miles away, and popping, snapping, squealing, swishing, crackling, and whirring noises were heard three hundred miles away as the turbulence behind the fireball generated extremely low-frequency electromagnetic energy which in turn introduced vibrations into nearby objects. Coyotes stopped howling, birds stopped singing, and animals ran for cover.

Perhaps our end will not come from flood, or famine, or fire, or disease, or even war. A large rock from space will do just fine. Did the native people sense the importance of the sky in the origin of their land, and is that why the shamans' art was so connected with the sky? I had always thought that the mountains were driven from below by molten heat, shifting continents, and time, that the clock of earth ticked for millions of years measured in intervals of ice, rain, wind, and sun, but in a cataclysmic instant the sky fell, the clock was smashed, and time began again.

SEVEN

Lake Abert: The Inland Sea

Upon these realms of salt,
upon these terraces of lake,
memories of washed mountains,
floods of spring, wind flows,
water ebbs, eons of memories.

N
O MATTER HOW OFTEN I approach the lake, I am astonished by the steep rock cliff rising two thousand feet above the eastern edge of the lake. The rim continues mile after mile, leaving only a narrow, boulder-strewn margin between the cliff and the salt-encrusted lake edge. Today the lake is more salty than the sea: a small inland sea only fifteen feet deep with sixty-four square miles of surface area and no outlet. During the last ice age of the Pleistocene, it was part of a larger inland lake covering much of south-central Oregon and given the name Lake Chewaucan. (Chewaucan is an Indian word meaning "place of roots or bulbs," a reference to the wetlands remaining after Pleistocene Lake Chewaucan dried.) Ten thousand years or more ago, the water of Lake Chewaucan covered the present Lake Abert to a depth of almost three hundred feet.

Caves were cut by waves near the edge of this vast ancient lake, and were inhabited as far back as thirteen thousand years before present. Near the outcropping known as Fort Rock, the lake dwellers lived in a wave-cut cave, wore sandals made of sagebrush, used a variety of stone implements, and enjoyed a lakeside view of a body of fresh water edged with tules and filled with fish and waterfowl. In 1938 the cave was excavated and the sandals carbon-dated by Dr. Luther Cressman, the man who would become known as the father of Oregon archaeology because of this

Abert Rim and Lake Abert, a classic example of horst-and-graben topography. *(Melvin Adams)*

discovery. His findings pushed the date of native habitation back so far that the textbooks had to be rewritten. Since then, discoveries at other sites in North and South America have pushed back the date of first inhabitancy even further by tens of thousands of years—according to certain archaeologists. But the scientists are wrong, in the eyes of Chief Weewa of the Paiute tribe. He believes that his people were always present in eastern Oregon and that they did not arrive via a land bridge from Asia.

Dr. Cressman's research showed that the people living on Lake Chewaucan ate a diverse diet reflecting the diversity and abundance of nature: thirty-six types of animals, forty different birds, seven types of insects, and forty seed types, not to mention fish. The animals consumed included horse, camel, and bison. Some have jokingly speculated that the animals were so abundant and unafraid of man that the natives practically walked up and built a fire under them to cook dinner. Were the native hunters in part responsible for the extinction of the large animals after the Pleistocene? Certainly the camel and horse were extinct by seventy-five hundred years before present, and bison were gone from eastern Oregon before white contact.

Since the last ice age, general drying has occurred, with some intermissions, leaving Lake Abert as a saline remnant of the former massive Lake Chewaucan. During this time, the habitation at Lake Abert has waxed and waned between nomadic hunters in the drier periods and permanent villages in the wetter climes. At the time of European contact, the Paiute population was probably about twenty-five square miles per person, according to Cressman. Nevertheless the evidence is strong that permanent villages existed and flourished on the shores of Lake Abert for extended periods since the last ice age. When the Oregon Highway Department conducted surveys along the eastern shore of the lake, 441 circular features were found, indicating the presence of dwellings or structures. The typical dwelling probably consisted of original stones or boulders supplemented with stacked stones of basalt. Its opening faced east with a petroglyph on a stone inside the circle on the south side. Grinding surfaces, which still remain, were often included on stones in the circle. The circles were up to twenty feet in diameter and about five feet high and were probably covered with brush or mats to form a conical roof. On surveying the thirteen miles of the eastern shore of the lake, the archaeologist Richard Pettigrew stated, "As I clambered over the rocks, finding yet another such site around each bend, my normal restraint slipped away and I found myself shouting and gasping with incredulity." I have personally found many of the stone circles and the petroglyphs in or near them. It is hard for me to imagine living in the rocks near the eastern edge of the lake; I have never remembered visiting the lake without experiencing an unceasing wind.

One of the first Europeans to see Lake Abert and record his observations was Peter Ogden. In May of 1827 he and his party of thirty-five men traveled along the east side of the lake bearing north, looking for beaver. Later, his friend, John Work of the Hudson's Bay Company, would travel along the west side of the lake heading south, also looking for beaver. Work's journal gives some flavor of the conditions encountered:

> October 16, Stormy, cold weather. Continued our journey $6^1/2$ hours, 20 miles W.S.W to Salt Lake (Lake Abert). No water to (be) found sooner. This was a most fatiguing day both on men and horses, particularly the horses. The greater part of the road was very stony which has several of them lame. We found good water in a small spring at the side of the lake.

John Work applied the name "Salt Lake" to what would be renamed Lake Abert by the later explorer John C. Fremont.

Fremont passed the lake while traveling northward on his legendary second western exploration for the United States Topographic Engineers. In his party was a remarkably diverse group which would prefigure the multiethnic history of the West: thirty-nine men, mostly Metis and French Canadian, including a free black man, Jacob Dodson; two Delaware Indian scouts; legendary mountain man Thomas Fitzpatrick as a guide; and famous scout Kit Carson. In later years, Fremont would be instrumental in wresting California from Mexico, be court martialled for mutiny, run for U.S. president unsuccessfully as a Republican candidate, be reinstated in the army, fight as a general in the Civil War, become wealthy from gold on his California estate, and serve as governor of Arizona. Along the way he would also save Kit Carson's life in an Indian battle in northern California. Always against slavery, Fremont remarked on the fine performance of Dodson during the second expedition to the West. A national forest named for Fremont today bounds the high, timbered, faulted mountain blocks on both sides of the Goose Lake basin in the Oregon desert, including much of the land in the Warner Mountains.

Kit Carson would later be noted for his relentless pursuit and slaughter of the Navajo, the burning of their villages and orchards, and the forced march to the concentration camp of the Bosque Redondo in New Mexico. Despite his brutal treatment of the natives, Carson to this day remains a hero in American folklore, claiming even a recent commemorative postage stamp in his honor. It was small justice that the Paiutes managed to steal a horse from him in his sojourn with Fremont through the Oregon desert.

Fremont's journal throws additional light on the early appearance of Lake Abert.

> December 20. (1843)—Traveling for a few hours down the stream this morning (Chewaucan River), we turned a point on the hill on our left, and came suddenly in sight of another and much larger lake, which, along its eastern shore, was closely bordered by the high black ridge which walled it in by a precipitous face on this side. Throughout this region the face of the country is characterized by these precipices of black volcanic rock, generally enclosing the valleys of streams, and frequently terminating in the hills.... Spread out over a length of 20 miles, the lake, when we, first came in view, presented a handsome sheet of water; and I gave to it the name of Lake Abert, in honor of the chief of the corps to which I belonged.... We were following an Indian trail which led along the steep rocky precipice; a black ridge along the western shore holding out no prospect whatever. The white efflorescences which lined the shore like a bank of snow, and the disagreeable odor which filled the air as soon as we came near, informed us too plainly that the water belonged to one of those fetid salt lakes which are common in this region.... There were flocks of ducks on the lake, and frequent tracks of Indians along

the shore, where the grass had been recently burnt by their fires....
December 22.—Today we left this forbidding lake.

Fremont decided to name the lake after his superior, Col. J.J. Abert. There is no evidence that Abert ever saw it or even visited the Oregon desert. Fremont's maps and journals were published with help from his well-connected wife and became classic references for many of the pioneers who began to move west after his expeditions. There is no evidence that Fremont himself ever returned to the region where he named so many features, including Winter Ridge, Summer Lake, and Lake Abert. It is a testament to the thoroughness of the destruction of one culture by another that the topography is named for people who visited the region briefly or not at all while nothing is named for the people who lived on the land for thousands of years.

Because it has no outflow and rarely dries up completely, Lake Abert is more salty than the sea and far more salty than other lakes in the Oregon desert. The dissolved solids in the lake approach 55,900 parts per million compared with 34,500 for the sea. Over ninety-nine percent of the dissolved solids in the lake are composed of sodium and potassium. Since the only major stream entering the lake is the Chewaucan River, what is the source of the salt? Reports prepared by scientists Kenneth Phillips and Van Denbaugh, who surveyed the lake, suggest several sources, including dry alkali dust blowing in the prevailing wind from Summer Lake to the west, minerals contributed by ephemeral streams such as Poison Creek draining into the lake, and input from numerous springs on the lake's west side. Salt is lost by precipitation to the lake bottom where it is covered with mud, forming a bottom that does not leak. The lake, in fact, presents an interesting example of the balances everywhere at work in nature. A precipitation of twelve inches a year contrasts with an evaporation of thirty-nine inches a year, the balance maintained by an inflow of ten thousand acre-feet from the Chewaucan River. No water is lost to leakage or outflow. When a drier than normal period occurs, the balance is upset, and the lake dries out completely. This happened once in the twentieth century, in the summer of 1924. The lake almost went dry six other years of the century.

Only living things tolerant to salt, heat, cold, dry wind, and gritty spray can live where the air temperature can range sixty degrees in a day and the humidity can vary between one hundred percent at night and zero percent during the day. The high elevation, clear air, and intense ultraviolet light allow only the most hardy life to live on rock, boulder, and salty shore. But because of its salinity, Lake Abert is enormously productive of salt-tolerant organisms, including brine shrimp—*Artemia salina*—and brine flies. In summer, vast quantities of algae float in the water along with diatoms in their microscopic cases of glass. The amount of brine shrimp approaches 14.5 million tons per year. In autumn, the shores are lined with rows of larval skins from emerging brine flies, the skins providing a rich protein source for migrating birds, including one hundred thousand grebes and ninety thousand phalarops. The lake also supports the largest nesting population of western snowy plovers in Oregon if not the world. The plover is likely to be listed as an endangered species because of loss of habitat in its coastal Oregon and California nesting areas. Many people traveling Highway 395 along the east edge of the lake consider the land to be barren and devoid of life, not knowing the tremendous fecundity in the waters nearby.

The biological proliferation does not stop at the lake's edge. On the boulders and rocks a colorful and healthy population of lichens flourishes. If clean air and longevity are important to the size and brightness of a lichen, the Lake Abert lichens have lived in a pristine atmosphere for a very long time. Other plants contribute to the scene including sage, juniper, rabbitbrush, and greasewood. Once the plant life was even more diverse. Desert allocarya, Columbia cress, and long-flowered snowberry have either disappeared or are threatened in the lake basin. The Bureau of Land Management has recently adopted plans to reintroduce, inventory, and sustain these species.

Today the federal government, which owns most of Lake Abert, manages it as an Area of Critical Environmental Concern. Objectives include managing the lake to support a host of sensitive species, including the peregrine falcon, long-billed curlew, California bighorn sheep, loggerhead shrike, pygmy rabbit, white-tailed antelope, ground squirrel, white-tailed jackrabbit, and Oregon lakes tui chub. A proposal by the Oregon Natural Desert Association to make part of the north Abert Rim region a wilderness area is under consideration. Plans to convert the lake to a soda ash mine and a peak hydraulic pump power station have been suspended, but, in a sparsely populated region desperate for jobs, it is never entirely clear whether the last of the natural heritage will be exchanged for a few dollars. The extraction mentality has never led to permanent progress or the dreamed-of wealth sought in the Oregon desert, but its hold is irresistible and alive and well in the European mythology of the West.

   While sitting near the shore of Lake Abert in the incessant wind, it is possible to imagine the rim and boulders dissolving and bending in time like a clock in a Salvador Dali painting. The basalt that the Indians believed was animated with spirit yields in the mind to the soft texture of algae, fungi, bird feather, hollow bone, hair, and hide. The color of rabbitbrush and lichen erupts: small volcanoes of sentience. The elemental brine shrimp, glass-housed diatoms, and larval shell flies are consumed by birds and transformed into bone and sinew able to take off and fly thousands of miles in migration, heeding the cycles of seasonal tilt and solar orbit. The raw elements energize creation, and only our words, science, and illusions maintain our fragile and dissolving certainty long enough to keep us from being swept up into the sky with the clouds, birds, and currents of air.

EIGHT

Halophytes and Xerophytes

In a far place,
on unnamed lakes,
the world becomes
flesh
from salt, sun, water, wind.

I AM ASTONISHED BY plants and animals living on the high desert: plants able to grow on solid rock faces, miniature flowers blooming on rim rock shelves and rock flats with no apparent soil, tiny organisms thriving in hot springs and brines saltier than the ocean. How can living things survive such extremes of hot and cold, wet and dry, brine and fresh, rock and sand, calm and wind blast? I can think of no more demanding home, not even a tidal pool.

My astonishment was heightened one spring day at Petroglyph Lake. It was a wet spring, but the lake was in the process of drying. A zone of mud cracks extended completely around the lake's perimeter. As I walked along the edge, hundreds then thousands of tiny green and black frogs began to seep and ooze from every crack in the mud. The proliferation of frogs continued around the entire lake. I could not imagine so much fecundity in such a barren place as an ephemeral lake on a sage flat with no trees or cover. There are years when the lake is completely dry, meaning that this species of frog must cuddle beneath cracked mud for months on end. Later in the day, I walked north to find an unnamed lake on the map. Temporarily lost, I found it by the cacophony of frog song drifting on the brisk north wind. It was likely that every drying lake on the Oregon desert was teeming with frogs that spring day.

Of the desert plants able to withstand extreme conditions, lichens are the most intriguing to me. The bright red lichens near the shore of Lake Abert and other equally colorful lichens throughout the region manage to thrive on bare basalt rock faces, directly exposed to the intense high-altitude sun as well as the incessant winds which can bring bitter cold one hour and scorching heat the next. The lichen represents a true symbiosis or partnership of two plants: a fungus and an algae. Neither plant could live alone on a rock face: the algae possesses chlorophyll and makes sugar nutrients from the ingredients of sunlight, water, and carbon dioxide from the air; the fungus disposes of waste, absorbs water vapor from the air, and furnishes a sturdy matrix for attachment to the rock. No wonder lichens are called "pioneer" plants: the first plants able to grow in a given place. Eventually they reduce rock to soil over many generations. Although lichens are thought to reproduce sexually, the most expedient way to spread is simply for pieces to break off and be carried away by wind or animals. It is likely that individual lichens live as long as humans, but they require very clean air, and some lichens are sensitive indicators of air pollution.

Almost as amazing as lichens are the tiny desert flowers that bloom on the lithosol or rock-soil of the desert, which develops in areas underlain by basalt. Not even sage grows well on the lithosol. It seems that wherever even a teaspoon of soil accumulates between rock fragments, the flowers—some almost microscopic—bloom in a wet spring. The plants need to be small and close to the ground to survive the drying wind and lack of water on the lithosol.

In general, arid zone plants exhibit a number of adaptations: very strong osmotic or water-sucking potential due to high internal salt concentrations; waxy coatings called cuticles to save water loss; hairy leaves to reduce air movement and evaporation over the leaves; the ability to close stomata, the openings beneath the leaves, during the day to conserve water; reduction of leaf area compared to leaf volume; and the capacity to store water in the plant structures. Some larger desert plants like the sage and juniper release a toxin from the decaying material they shed to prevent other plants from growing under or near them. Why allow competitors to take precious water? This advantage, along with a shallow and spreading root system covering a large area and a deep tap root system, enables water harvesting from the brief and infrequent storms and extraction of water deep in the ground.

The saline zone near alkali playa lakes is even more extreme for plant growth than the lithosol zone. Here the plants must also adapt to high salt concentrations in addition to the problems of the lithosol plants.

Extreme salt-tolerant plants such as shadscale, greasewood, and saltgrass, the true halophyte, grow where no other plants can, and they do it by maintaining very high internal salt concentrations.

Halophytes are not restricted to plants of the saline zone near the lakes. Brine shrimp thrive in the salty waters of Lake Abert. These crustaceans are so tiny that it takes six thousand of them to make a pound, yet some years they are so prolific in Lake Abert that their tiny brown eggs or cysts float in visible rafts. The sexually produced cysts are so resistant to drying that they have survived in lab beakers full of dry mud for fifteen years, only to bounce back to life when water is added. These tiny shrimp feed by filtering plankton and algae from the water, swim by waving their tiny articulated appendages, and respire by removing oxygen from the salt water through their body walls. Brine shrimp are transparent organisms, but they change color to match the color of their latest meal. The proliferation of high-protein brine shrimp in Lake Abert has not gone unnoticed by flocks of thousands of migrating birds including grebes, phalarops, and plovers.

It seems appropriate that the sagebrush, that icon of the desert habitat, itself something of a halophyte and xerophyte, is given the genus name *Artemisia* after the Greek virgin goddess Artemis, the goddess of the hunt and wild nature. The wild gods and goddesses of the natural world seem alive and well in the Oregon desert, and not even the hardest rock, the saltiest water, the driest wind, nor the longest drought can deter their ingenious proliferation.

———

NINE

Atmospheric

Curtains of virga
spilled down,
swaths of wind
scattered the sunlight.
Just before sunset, a
yellow hole opened
and poured light.

T HE CLOUDS AND SUNSETS of the Oregon desert left such an impression
on me that when I left home to go to college, I was determined to
be a weatherman. For a time, I did major in meteorology. Although I have
lived since in many places in the West, the atmosphere of eastern Oregon
still engages my imagination.

The climate and weather of the desert directly reflects the topography of the land. The prevailing storm track and jet stream from the Pacific Ocean bring storms directly perpendicular to the north-south
oriented mountain ranges. The prevailing tracks are so strong that for all
my years growing up in the desert, I can scarcely even remember an east
wind. The storms from the west, already depleted by their encounter with
the Cascade Range, are forced up and over the ridges: an effect the meteorologists call orographic uplift. The result is expanding and cooling air.
If the rising air is cooled to the dew point, spectacular cloud structures and sunsets result. The cloud formations are particularly startling in the open sage country where trees, fog, and mist seldom
obscure the view. The mile-high air only adds to the clarity of the light.

My acquaintance with fog had to await arrival at college on the west side of the Cascade Range.

Often the winds rising over the faulted rim rocks form layered or lenticular clouds that look like stacked, upside-down bowls. The clouds are often so high that a bright multicolor light show ensues as the clouds change hue with the varying angles of the setting sun. Lenticular clouds are favored by sailplane pilots seeking to break altitude and distance records by catching the up-thrusting layers of air that often extend hundreds of miles north to south along the mountain ranges of the Great Basin, but if parallel layers begin to sheer because a layer begins moving faster than a layer below it, gyres of turbulent air form. If the gyres cool to the dew point, visible comma-shaped or wave clouds result. And if the gyres are not visible, aircraft can unexpectedly encounter extremely turbulent air on a perfectly clear day. More than one light plane pilot has been caught and killed downwind of a fault range by an encounter with a gyre while flying too low. The ride up one side of a gyre can be quite exhilarating, but the ride down the other can be deadly.

On a smaller scale and closer to the ground, the orographic winds of west-facing Abert Rim are a hang glider's dream come true. It is said that you cannot throw a hat off the rim because the wind will bring it back to your hand like a boomerang, a theory I tested when surveying roads near Abert Rim during my college days. (I had to do a little climbing to get my hat back, but the experiment was a partial success.) Already one hang glider pilot has lost his life testing the rim rock winds of the Oregon desert.

My own flying experience with the updrafts of Abert Rim and the Warner Mountains revolved around my fascination with airplanes. During high school, I would often work at the Lakeview airport washing and fueling planes in exchange for rides and lessons. Much to the chagrin of the airport operator and flying instructor, a World War II veteran flyer named Myron Buswell, I would sometimes ride with another World War II veteran named Dave Glass. Glass had a 1930s vintage Taylorcraft, a two-seat (side-by-side), fabric-covered aircraft with long wings. In fact, the Taylorcraft had much more wing than engine; it was really a powered glider. Glass had survived the war as a tail gunner in B-17 bombers, and the experience made him a little reckless in the eyes of the other pilots at the field. He would take me up, cut the engine near Abert Rim, and soar for hours at a time. He had a reputation for staying airborne much longer than his fuel supply would allow, but in reality he was simply riding the thermals and rim updrafts of Lake County. I stopped going up with Glass when Buswell threatened to tell my parents about my adventures.

In summer and spring when the uplifted air is unstable due to thermal heating from the earth, lines of thunderstorms form along the ridges. Riding horses one day at the top of the Steens Mountains, we watched the thunderstorms building below us to the west all morning, but by noon the ridge became dangerous with no cover or trees. After a wet, exciting gallop to a cabin, I vowed never again to be caught on a barren ridge on a horse in a thunderstorm.

Microbursts or downpours of wind, rain, and hail from the bottoms of mature thunderstorm clouds are vivid on the desert because of the excellent visibility. It is possible to be standing in warm, bright sunshine while watching a falling, streaked fountain of air and water drop from the bottom of a cloud just a few hundred yards away. When the downpour of air hits the ground and spreads outward in violent gusts, the pleasant afternoon sun quickly scurries away to be replaced within a minute by a cold, raw wind not unlike that of a winter blizzard. It is possible to be hot, sunburned, and thirsty, then soaked, cold, and dry again all within the same hour.

During summer and spring days when the grass and sage flats are warm and thermal air currents are about but the air is not so unstable as to foster thunderstorms, the dust devil makes its appearance. Contrary to a number of weather books which state that dust devils rotate clockwise, I have seen them spin in both directions. On the Oregon desert, they are also larger and stronger than those described in books, and they are sometimes invisible. More than once, a pleasant day in camp has been disrupted by a sudden cyclone of wind flattening the tents, turning over tables and chairs, and spilling food and camp gear on the ground. In the spring there is simply little dust for the devils to pick up, particularly after a wet winter when the desert is well-anchored with grass and flowers. In the fall or in a dry year when there is plenty of dust, sand, and tumbleweeds to move around, a direct encounter with a devil can be quite painful. Dust devils—or should we call these salt devils?—are, on the other hand, invariably visible on playa lake edges and alkali flats where much fine alkali dust is ready to be blown away. Some scientists think that blowing alkali dust picked up from Summer Lake and deposited in Lake Abert to the east is a major contributor to the high salinity of the latter.

Of the atmospheric phenomena in the desert, the most romantic, beautiful, and intriguing remains for me the virga. When a cumulonimbus thunderstorm cloud or less-aggressive cumulus cloud drops sheets of air, rain, or snow in an atmospheric waterfall, sometimes the air beneath the cloud is dry enough to evaporate the moisture before it touches the ground. Streaks of rain called virga dance beneath the cloud, flirting with and teasing the dry ground. The effect is not unlike that of a belly dancer in an old Hollywood movie teasing the sultan in his harem tent. In Latin, one of the definitions of virga is "a magic wand" of Mercury. This definition fits well the magical weather sculptures, the abstract cloud art, and the tantalizing streaks of rain in the high desert.

At Long Lake, there is a petroglyph that I believe is a depiction of twin storm gods. Their large, goggle eyes may have flashed in the lightning of the minds of their artist creators; their outstretched arms appear to have containers of pouring rain beneath them. Could it be that the ancient shamans of the desert were also beguiled by virga?

TEN

Sunstones

*Each thundering season
is remembered,
a silent bell rings in stone.*

THE SAGE-COVERED GROUND near the Rabbit Hills sparkles: thousands of small crystals flash in the sun. Mineral gems called sunstones, the Oregon State gemstone, lie scattered across the desert floor.

The sunstone is found only in two places in the world, both in the high desert of Oregon: Harney County and Lake County near Adel. The feldspar sunstone gems originated in a hot magma mass: a lava furnace of eleven hundred degrees. The gems were inclusions or phenocrysts which cooled slower than the surrounding lava, allowing the crystals time to grow as large as three inches across. They become exposed at the ground because the basalt rock around them is more erodible. Most of the stones are clear, but red, blue, and green ones are also found more rarely. Tiny copper flakes in the crystal reflect sunlight and give the stones a unique metallic glitter or shimmer called aventurescence.

Today, at the Lake County site, a few camp trailers and small backhoes sit on private mines next to the public collection area; the owners pursue a modest dream of extractive wealth in the coyote- and rattlesnake-infested sage. Even the natives apparently collected and traded sunstones; they are found in Native American collections on the west side of Oregon.

The area near the Lake County sunstone site was once the scene of more ambitious dreams of wealth. In 1891 a modest gold rush occurred and a town called Dyson City was incorporated and platted. Later, in 1908, the town of Goldrun was incorporated, but not a trace of either town or even a miner's cabin remains. Some think that Rabbit Creek or Foley Creek near the Rabbit Hills was the crossing of the lost Meek wagon train in 1845. Joe and Stephen Meek, cousins of President James Polk, came west as trappers and mountain men. Stephen, the less experienced of the two, offered to take an immigrant train via an eastern Oregon route that would save the treacherous raft trip down the Columbia River to the Dalles. He became lost with serious results; at one point, over a period of three days, three people died. When the train reached safety, a blue bucket full of gold nuggets was noticed. The nuggets had been collected by a young girl from a stream crossed along the way, but the blue-bucket mine was never relocated. Most historians place the crossing and the lost mine much further north in eastern Oregon than Rabbit Creek, but an obscure manuscript in the Lake County Library by a relative of one of the train's survivors makes the case for the "mine" location at or near the Rabbit Hills.

The sunstone deposits are only one manifestation of the unique volcanic landscape of the Oregon high desert. In July 1959, a new continuous geyser erupted near Adel, sending two-hundred-degree water 150 feet into the air—a recent indication of the many hot springs and underground thermal energies scattered throughout Lake County. Further east at Lakeview a geyser known as "Old Perpetual" had been active many years; although it was not spouting when John Work camped near the site in 1832, he did note in his journal hot springs containing skulls and bones of the natives who inhabited the region. Today a number of homes and businesses in Lakeview are heated by geothermal water, but the great potential of this power source remains largely untapped throughout Lake County.

My memories of these hot springs extend to the historic mineral pool located in an old shed-like structure near Paisley. My grandmother lived near the bathhouse for years, and it was a favorite weekend drive in the winter if the roads were clear. Steam rose so thick from the water that it was hard to even see the water's surface. About twenty minutes in the pool was all one could stand, but the skin emerged as soft and shiny as if anointed with a fine powder. The rough-hewn wooden walls of the bathhouse contain the carved initials of visitors and lovers going back decades; my own initials have been there for almost fifty years. According to historians, the house started as simply a hollow log for the buckaroos and sheepherders to bathe in before the shed was built. It is conceivable that the Indians bathed there even before the cowboys discovered the springs.

The Warner Valley near Adel was also the location of "earthquake swarms" unique in recent history. In May and June of 1968, over 122 earthquakes occurred in the valley, the largest exceeding 5 on the Richter scale. According to geologists Richard Couch and Stephen Johnson, "the earthquake epicenters suggest that the blocks forming the central graben moved down relative to the blocks forming the east wall." The subterranean gods of horst-and-graben country continue to play building blocks with huge masses of rock, and our foundations shake, reminding us of our tenuous hold on the land.

In north Lake County are two large craters, one and one-half miles in diameter and one mile in diameter, respectively. Both look like the result of good-sized meteors striking the earth, but the cause is found beneath the earth rather than in the sky. When a hot magma mass intrudes into a lake or beneath a lake shore, a catastrophic explosion of steam and hot gas can be expected, resulting in craters and rock formations called maars. There are fifteen maars in Lake County; the Hole-in-the-Ground and Big Hole craters are examples of simple maars that date back five to ten million years to the Pliocene.

Not content to blow large craters in the ground, create earthquake swarms, heat water, and erupt geysers, the subterranean furnaces of Lake County also threw out blobs of molten lava near Glass Buttes, creating a unique type of obsidian found nowhere else on earth. Obsidian itself is common, forming when lava cools very rapidly, not allowing time for a crystal structure to grow. But Glass Buttes' iridescent or opalescent obsidian called Chatoyant was formed when the spherical blobs or "bombs" of lava rotated while traveling through the air. The crystals inside the bomb were still in a plastic state when they hit the earth; the impact caused them to fracture, bend, distort. The resulting gem-quality obsidian displays prismatic, shimmering colors. Besides the Chatoyant obsidian, Glass Buttes also contains red-and-black banded, golden, bluish-silver, red, and jet black obsidian stones.

At Long Lake far south of Glass Buttes, several of us found a cache of large obsidian fragments and a spear point which were clearly of the unique colors and structure of obsidian from Glass Buttes. The circular cache on the lake floor may have been deposited when a hunter's tule raft sank or capsized. Glass Buttes' obsidian arrowheads have been found in the Southwest and far to the east, a testament to the extensive trading routes that existed before white contact. Glass Buttes were virtual "quarries" to the native peoples. Obsidian needles up to seven inches long were reported by aged Indians, the needlelike forms being used for ornamentation.

In north Lake County the lava flows also created long, tunnel-like lava tube caves. The air in the caves is so dense and cold that they provided the early settlers with a source of ice. More than one pioneer Sunday ice cream social was held at South Ice Cave near Christmas Valley. The tubes were formed when the top crust of a lava flow cooled first, creating a solid roof while the lava below continued to flow away, leaving behind a tunnel. In addition, near the South Ice Cave site, a deep, narrow rift two miles long was formed as a tension fracture in basalt about one thousand years ago. This fracture, called Crack-in-the-Ground, also trapped cold air and preserved winter ice.

In the desert are stones that flash in the sun, explosive craters, erupting geysers and hot pools, swarms of earthquakes, lost and abandoned gold, bombs of glittering obsidian glass, and tubes of frozen lava. The gems and nuggets sparkle and beckon us to the underworld with promises of wealth. The earth shakes, fractures, cracks, and spews. The gods of the underworld threaten to throw about blocks of earth as it was in the beginning. We go about our lives, but our feet tread close to the refiner's fire, closer than we care to know. The molten heart of the earth boils and seethes and throws out little suns encased in crystal. The earth, a star remnant, accumulates star dust. A pantheon of gods lives in the desert today: a gathering of fire, water, wind, and salt.

ELEVEN

Netting the Sun

The cosmos of the mind
harvests the sky
gathering black holes,
big bangs, quasars,
and novas
as if plucking
flowers from Van Gogh's
starry fields.

There are over one hundred petroglyph sites in the high desert of Lake County. Some of the sites are confined to one boulder, but the most extensive site extends along rim rock for five miles and contains over three thousand designs. The sites are on long, low basalt rim rocks or large boulders near the edges of ephemeral, ancient lake beds. A few sites are located near springs or in the mountain passes between lake beds.

It is difficult to know the tribal membership of the shamans who made the rock art in the Oregon desert because different tribes used the area at different historical times and in different parts of the year. The older petroglyphs, perhaps dating as far back as ten thousand years, may have been made by ancestors of what are now the Modoc and Klamath tribes. The Achomawi or Pit River tribe also used parts of the region. Some anthropologists think that the Paiute tribe displaced the Modocs and Klamaths to the west out of the desert country about one thousand years ago.

It is known that most petroglyphs were made by scraping or pecking the host rock to break through the dark patina or weathered crust on the rock face. A few examples of pictograms or painted rock art also survive. The painted forms were made using ground minerals bound by animal fats and plant extracts.

Numerous theories exist as to the meaning of the petroglyphs: the art was made to foster hunting magic and the success of the hunt; to record astronomical observations; to mark trails and water holes, art as maps; it was a mnemonic device to train young hunters or the artistic rendering of the sacred experience of the shamans. Perhaps these questions will never be answered with scientific certainty, but for me the petroglyphs have a visceral impact. They exude mystery and magic. They seem surprisingly akin to the art of children and modern artists like Klee and Miro, who never saw them.

On a rim rock facing eastward overlooking the juniper- and sage-filled canyon of Rabbit Creek is a petroglyph site extending for over a mile. Hundreds of designs including circular and rectangular net patterns are found on the smooth rock faces. Similar patterns appear at Long Lake and at other sites in the region. At first I thought the nets were simple depictions of spider webs or perhaps the patterns a shaman would see in his mind during the initial stages of a trance flight induced by hallucinogens, deprivation, or drumming. But the drawings are far from random patterns and seem to be an ordered metaphor or symbol. Because of the high location of the site with an uncluttered eastern horizon before it, the eye is drawn to the sky. The interpretation became clear after I read a journal article by John Rafter on sun-and-net designs in the Southwest. Suddenly, the Rabbit Creek patterns appeared to be nets that have caught the sun.

It is important to understand that the summer and winter solstices were critical times for the original inhabitants of the desert. In the winter, the sun rose lower and lower in the sky each day, threatening to not come up at all. In the summer was the opposite concern; the sun appeared higher and higher in the sky each day, dangerously overheating the dry earth.

According to Rafter and other writers, certain California tribes used a net-like figure to symbolize the Milky Way. The net resembled a chain of diamonds or zigzag lines crossing each other. Because the Milky Way intersects the rising sun at the summer and winter solstices, the net representation held particular importance. The Milky Way was the home of the dead and the great spirits, and this notion only enhanced the importance of the net symbol. In the mythology of certain tribes, the Milky Way net caught the sun to prevent it from rising higher at the summer solstice, while at the winter solstice the net prevented the sun from disappearing.

A shaman site near the town of Adel, Oregon, on the high desert.
(*Melvin Adams*)

To arrest the sun at the solstices, the Modoc and other tribes of northern California utilized the hoop-and-net game. To play the game, hoops representing the sun were rolled along the ground much as the sun rolls across the sky from season to season. To stop the sun, the hoops were pegged with a hooked pole or sun stick. The stick was used to symbolically hook the sun and pull it back into the sky at winter solstice or back down from the sky at summer solstice.

Did ancient people create and then place spiritual power "out there"? Did they separate the great spirit and nature, or themselves and nature, or art and nature? According to Jamie de Angulo, a pioneer doctor who lived with the Achomawi and studied their culture, everything around them had spiritual and practical power: animals, stars, wind, storms, the moon, rocks, springs, everything. They tried to know and gather this power into themselves in every way they could from all of its sources. They thought that humans and animals once spoke the same language and that the spirits of the dead became stars in the Milky Way.

I grew up in Lake County and thought I knew its geography, but I seldom noticed the petroglyphs despite all of my camping in the outback.

The early explorers, soldiers, ranchers, and miners did not note them in their journals. General Crook did not mention them in his autobiography even though his soldiers built a stone bridge across the narrows of Warner Lake within a stone's throw of a boulder field literally covered with petroglyphs. Modern writers like William Kittredge who grew up on ranches in Warner Valley do not mention them in their books. It is a statement about our own culture that only now is the ancient art of the Oregon desert being noticed.

Someone said that the longer we live in the West, the more like the natives we will become. Australian aboriginals claim that it is impossible to possess a foreign territory because in the territory live the spirits of the native inhabitants who reincarnate in new-born children. Or perhaps Swiss psychologist Carl Jung is right that the unconscious of the conqueror eventually finds and accepts the primitive unconscious of the native. Perhaps this is why the iconography found on petroglyphs appears so often in the work of modern artists and children.

TWELVE

A Star Explodes

Watch towers
beacons and steeples
lift the roof of night.
The dark does not come.

O<small>N</small> J<small>ULY</small> 5, 1054 A.D., a startling event occurred in the heavens, an event certain to have been noticed by the sky-oriented shamans of the Oregon desert. Because it took place during the usually clear skies of summer, the tribe may have become alarmed and sought the help of the shamans. The date of the event is known because it was recorded by Japanese and Chinese observers. Following close behind the summer solstice, the shamans would have been worried about another sun in the daytime sky at the very time efforts had been completed by hoop-and-net games or sun spearing to bring the sun down from its position of intense midsummer heat.

The event known to modern astronomers as a supernova or exploding star appeared in the constellation Taurus, an explosion that created what today is called the Crab Nebula. When viewed from western North America, the supernova would have been seen in close proximity to the crescent moon when the supernova was brightest on July 5. It would have been visible for twenty-three days during the daytime and gradually faded in the nighttime sky for hundreds of days after that.

In the Southwest, the supernova was viewed and recorded on rock at several sites, including the pueblo at Chaco Canyon; the event was shown as a crescent moon close to a tic-tac-toe symbol used to represent a star. At Lava Beds National Monument in northern California, the site of the

Examples of the complicated graphic language of the ancient Oregon desert shamans. *(Melvin Adams)*

Modoc War, a similar depiction was created in Fern Cave. To the east of the Lava Beds at Long Lake and at Petroglyph Lake, both in the Oregon desert, the shamans also may have recorded this important event on rock.

At the Long Lake site, about a dozen different rock panels apparently depict the supernova event, several of which resemble the Southwest and Lava Beds petroglyphs. Some of the Long Lake panels also appear to show, in the form of patterns of dots and slash marks, an astronomical enumeration of the days that the supernova was visible. One of the clearest and most intriguing panels depicts exactly twenty-three slash marks which end at a crescent moon symbol, and a line connected to a circular sun symbol points directly to the twenty-third slash mark. After the crescent moon symbol, additional marks perhaps depict the continued visibility of the supernova at night. Other panels at Long Lake appear to have arrays of about twenty marks, but they are extremely faded. (To my knowledge, the numerical depictions are not found at other supernova petroglyph sites in the West.) Still another panel at Long Lake, while without slash marks or dots, shows a stick-figure observer, a sun circle, a crescent moon, and two tic-tac-toe symbols for stars. Similar panels exist nearby at Petroglyph Lake, and it may be that other astronomical events are recorded by petroglyphs as well. For instance, at Abert Rim, a petroglyph appears to depict a comet, complete with curved tail.

Since it is unlikely that a dozen shamans were active at Long Lake at the same time, how is it possible to explain the many and varied representations of the same event at the same place? Perhaps the event was of such consequence that it became part of the sacred knowledge of the shamans to be passed on from one generation to another, a sort of supernova priesthood. Some of the panels could have been made later by descendent shamans to commemorate an important event seen by their ancestors. If this interpretation is correct, the Long Lake site is one of the important astronomical observatories in the West because of the number and variety of depictions of the exploding star event. It may also be unique because it records the event with patterns of dots and slashes, counts of the number of days the new sun was visible during the daytime.

The shamans, because of their orientation to the sky and its reflection in their petroglyphs, were the artists and astronomers of their time. The metaphors they created on rock are similar to the metaphors of modern artists and storytellers: exploding stars, flying animals, ascending humans, disembodied spirits. According to modern cosmologists, the universe began in an instant of searing creativity when matter expanded and cycled through star deaths and star births over and over again until large elements were fabricated piece by piece from fundamental particles. The matter concentrated to form planets around some stars, preparing the structure for life. Once sentient minds evolved, the universe could see itself through the mirror of pondering minds fashioned from incinerated dust and flux. With language these minds commanded into creation art, music, and science to celebrate.

Perhaps the shaman artists depicting the supernova knew at some elemental level the importance of star explosions and star dust in their own makeup. Did the furnaces of stellar matter engrave consciousness into the human mind as surely as carbon and nitrogen were forged in the exploding stars? Are the native peoples wrong when they consider rocks to be inhabited by spirit and the stars to be the souls of the dead?

THIRTEEN

The Stone Bridge

Behold, this stone shall be a witness unto us.
—Joshua 24:27

G ENERAL CROOK, a West Point graduate, Civil War veteran, and inveterate Indian fighter, in 1867 led a campaign to subdue hostile tribes of the northern Paiute in southern Oregon and northern California; later he took part in the Apache campaigns of the Southwest. Crook spent virtually his entire career in the West on Indian campaigns from Rouge River to Arizona. He was noted for his innovative use of Indian scouts, his ability as a fly fisherman, and his diplomatic skill in reaching treaties, though in his own words the natives of the Oregon high desert did not fare so well. "In returning to Old Warner, I found a band of Indians on a little lake, almost in site of Warner. We killed a lot of them." Today a peak in Lake County can be found on the maps: Crook Peak.

Crook used Fort Warner on top of Hart Mountain as the center of his operations, but winter at this site proved formidable. In one campaign near the fort, his soldiers almost froze to death in a blizzard; he himself would state that their beards were one mass of ice. In response to the hostile climate, he ordered the fort moved about forty-five miles west to the Warner Mountains, a more moderate location, but not much. Snow drifts and lack of supplies made access to the new Fort Warner so difficult that by the spring of 1868 some of the soldiers had scurvy. Crook left behind two soldiers at old Fort Warner, Edward Cantrell and Lewis Debold; their graves were finally marked in 1997.

Nevertheless, the new fort site was not without its merits. From the wonderful letters home of an officer's wife at the new Fort Warner during the period of November 1867 to September 1868, a literary picture emerges of life at the post. Julia Gilliss traveled with her husband by ship to Panama, by land across the isthmus of Panama, and then by ship to San Francisco and Portland. She, her baby, and her husband were posted at several forts in the Pacific Northwest. She describes the "imposing display" of the wagon train that took them across Oregon to Fort Warner: a train complete with soldiers, Mexican drivers, mules, and baggage wagons. When she arrived, she was one of five women at the post. She and her family first lived in plank shanties with dirt floors, her shanty being the only one with a glass window. By 1868 the situation improved to solid log houses with thatch roofs, "the warmest buildings imaginable." By that time a sawmill had been brought to the fort: the first in the history of Lake County. She described dinner parties and ice cream socials. "We are very comfortable here despite the snow wall between us and the outer world." At first she did not seem sympathetic to the Indians, but later she would say, "I think it is a wretched unholy warfare; the poor creatures are hunted down like wild beasts and shot down in cold blood." On one visit to the fort to conclude a treaty, the Indians showed so much interest in her baby, the "pale papoose," she was afraid they would steal the child. As Julia became more and more captured by the beauty of the Warner Mountains, her letters became poetic.

In order for General Crook to move Fort Warner to the new location in the Warner Mountains, it was necessary to first find a way across the Warner Lakes. The Warner Valley, located in a graben between faulted Hart Mountain to the east and the Warner Mountains to the west, was filled with a lake that Crook believed to be some seventy miles long and fifteen miles wide. But he had found a narrow neck in the lake only three or four hundred yards wide, and there he ordered his troops to build a stone causeway to support the crossing of wagons. The land as usual presented a challenge to military engineering: "after the weight of the rock remained on it for some time, it suddenly disappeared, rock and all. It seemed this ground was simply floating." The stone bridge was eventually completed, and today remnants of it are sometimes visible when the lake level is low.

Within a stone's throw of the bridge lies a field of basalt boulders, some as large as a house, that have rolled down from the steep, sheer face of Hart Mountain. On the smooth faces of the boulders are etched and painted the remarkable stories of the shamans who inhabited this land. Crook's soldiers no doubt camped among these very boulders, yet the artwork is not mentioned in any known journal of the period.

At the Stone Bridge petroglyph site, shamans in self-portraits appear to dance across the rock face as if in a series of drawings for an animated film. In one series, the shaman is shown with stick legs, round head, and stick horns. A transformation then occurs to a form with stick legs, amorphous feet, and large head with plumage. At the right of the sequence, the legs, plumage, feet, and neck all disappear while the globular body with small head appears to bounce into space like an inflated ball or bubble. The sequence is entirely consistent with the transformative phase of the shaman's astral journey wherein the shaman, according to Mircea Eliade, noted professor and authority on shamanism, changes to horned animal or plumed bird form, loses limbs, and takes flight in an immaterial and spiritual form.

In another series at the same site, a human-lizard form complete with head, phallus, and clawed, upraised arms and legs appears to leap upward as if boosted by some unseen force. Next to it, another form with visor face and horns appears to grab stars in each hand while leaping upward, propelled by spring-like feet. The form then appears to transform into a mountain sheep ascending at an angle upward, the swept-back horns only adding to the impression of speed and motion.

Another panel at Stone Bridge depicts a human-lizard form with a star grasped by a front limb. Nearby a mountain sheep form ascends vertically. Other more abstracted forms appear to move toward a cosmic portal represented by a circle with a central dot.

Other beings represented at the Stone Bridge site become even more fanciful. A monster with a star-figure head grasps a star in each of its forelimbs as if holding them aloft in the heavens. A pair of stick-figure limbs appears at mid-body while one back limb grasps a star. The other back limb becomes a line connecting to a portal or anchor of some type. Nearby a small insect-like creature with claw legs and six antennae seems to accompany the monster. The impression is of a fanciful, abstracted beast carrying stars around the heavens with such zest that a lifeline is necessary to anchor the being back to some reality. While in the trance state under the influence of deprivation and surrounded by space, isolation, wind, and animal calls, the shaman appears to have invented creatures into which to transform for mental flight into the heavens.

Another boulder at Stone Bridge contains an insect-like anthropomorph with large eyes, multiple plumes, and wavy mouth tentacles. The anthropomorph grasps a star portal as if trying to carry it like an egg back to some cosmic nest. Next to it, another creature with bowed stick-figure arms and legs sports a pendant dangling from a stick-figure ear. The ear pendant form, while rare in Lake County, is common on petroglyphs in the Southwest. (The pendant can be thought of as an antenna by which the shaman received the sounds associated with the trance-like flight.) A number of the figures at Stone Bridge resemble modern-day monsters from science fiction movies except that they leap into the heavens from star to star rather than from skyscraper to skyscraper.

Mountain sheep have been reintroduced to Hart Mountain and can sometimes be seen from the stone bridge site. Flocks of pelicans soar in endless circles in the hot thermals near the lake while flocks of ducks, geese, and shorebirds feed and rest in the shallow waters. An occasional dust devil breaks the silence with a swish of air. The intense light of the high, thin desert air casts a purple glow over rock and rim. The soldiers are gone, the shamans are gone, the stone bridge is nearly absorbed in the soft mud and salt of the lake, but strange creatures and animals leap from their inanimate rock forms and ascend into the sky.

PART THREE

REMNANTS

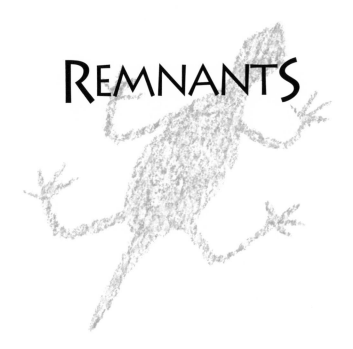

FOURTEEN

Aspen

For there is hope of a tree, if it be cut
down, that it will sprout again, and that the
tender branch thereof will not cease.
—Job 14:7

THEY GROW ALONG EPHEMERAL CREEKS in high desert canyons or near seeps and springs on the faulted mountain ridges. *Populus tremuloides* from the Latin means "people, a great number." I became attracted to them in childhood because of an isolated grove in Deep Creek Canyon near an old sheep-crossing bridge. The bridge was no longer maintained after the collapse of the vast sheep industry in Lake County. For many years after tumbling into Deep Creek, the log beams provided deep holes and cover for trout. Eventually the flood waters of numerous spring melts removed even the logs.

The sheep bridge aspen grove was a secret place far from any road, a place only for me and my father. We visited it to perform the sacred rituals of fly fishing for the native redband trout and to drink from the spring in the grove using a rusty tin can left hanging on a branch for that purpose. Seldom did we see other people in the canyon or even signs of them. The trek required fording Deep Creek, a difficult feat for a young boy, especially in the spring when the water was high. In the canyon we often encountered rattlesnakes, beaver, deer, hawks, swallows, and porcupine.

Beaver in particular revealed their presence with a few gnawed or downed aspen used for food, dams, and lodges. Although the beaver can eat prodigious amounts of aspen bark, they create new ground for aspen by damming the water and creating ponds which fill in with sediment.

We found a number of the ponds were particularly fine places to catch the larger, lazy trout of Deep Creek.

Our ritual drinking from the spring in the aspen grove was followed by a brief nap while we waited for the right hour when the sun was off the water and the trout active in the ripples and pools. The nap was enhanced by the sound of trembling aspen leaves and the pulsing gurgle and roar of Deep Creek as the water tumbled over and around boulders. The trip was best enjoyed in the fall when the leaves were turning, the creek low, and the trout anxious to stock up on flies for winter. In that season the air was crisp and the breezes brittle at times, breaking up the pockets of heat that accumulated in the canyon. The autumn light was like a flame charring the canyon walls in purple, red, and orange. It was like paradise. We would often tarry too long and have to negotiate the narrow, rocky trail and ford the creek in the dark. Sometimes we would camp in the grove, build a fire, and roast fresh trout in the coals.

I realize now that our pilgrimage to the grove, the ritual fishing and drinking of pure water, was really a baptismal rite and sacrament. Later I would feel the same way when taking the sacrament of bread and wine in church. Only the aspen grove ceremony was somehow more intense and real: the water colder, the music of the aspen leaves more sacred, the canyon walls more inspiring than a cathedral. I always had the strangest feeling that the aspen were people—lost souls, not unhappy, just a little sad to be encased in bark in the crystalline air of a deserted canyon. They felt like a family, a bit lonely but glad to see us once in awhile. I still have this feeling of friendship when visiting an aspen grove, and when I drink the spring water cleansed by their roots, it is like drinking their blood in remembrance.

Aspens in the Warner Mountains and in much of the West are really remnants. Because of the general drying since the last ice age, they have been pushed back into the moist seeps and spongy ground of high meadows and isolated canyons. Even though aspen can produce up to two million seeds a season, they rarely establish themselves in new areas by seed because they are so sensitive to drying at critical times in germination. Instead, they reproduce mostly by underground stems or suckers, which feed off the main root system of an established grove. Visible stems called ramets force themselves upward into the sunlight from the communal root system—much as the Native Americans of the region believed that they themselves emerged from the underworld. A grove is really a single tree; each "tree" or stem in the communal tree is a clone genetically like the rest of the grove. A single seed, if it does manage to germinate, is capable of producing up to forty-seven thousand stems or trees covering over one hundred acres. Genetically different groves can be distinguished by recognizable color boundaries in spring and fall. The communal root system of a distinct grove can conceivably live forever, but the individual stems of the clone live up to two hundred years. Fossil aspen leaves have been found that date back fifteen million years.

Branches break off the trees in the Deep Creek aspen grove, leaving what appear to be fluttering birds or eyes on the bark, as if souls contained in the tree are flying away while the rest of the family observes with the eyes of eternity. The initials my father and I carved in the bark are fading. I think of him and wonder if I should have placed his ashes here instead of in the cemetery next to my mother.

FIFTEEN

Pronghorn

I see vast flocks of birds
on glacial lakes, woolly beasts
prowl the borders, and spring
is ten thousand miles away.

When the first explorers, cavalry soldiers, and cattle men arrived on the ranges of the Oregon desert, it was in the words of David Shirk, "A stockman's paradise." At that time the desert had not been overgrazed for a hundred years by cattle and sheep, nor had the range fires been suppressed, nor had the pronghorn antelope herds been reduced almost to extinction, nor the bighorn sheep totally eliminated. (Only in recent years have the bighorn sheep been reintroduced to the Oregon desert.) Shirk and other early European immigrants describe the desert as a bunch-grass prairie, with sage present but far less dominant than now. The foreign, annual weeds of Russian thistle and cheatgrass had not yet invaded the disturbed lands, suppressing the native, perennial grasses and shrubs. The bunch grasses grew as high as the belly of a horse, and the rocks and soil on the ground were covered with a spongy, velvety mass of plants called cryptogams: mosses, fungi, and algae. Cryptogams absorbed the infrequent moisture from rain or snow, stored it, and released it to the tiny desert flowers, the bunch grasses, and shrubs. Once the cryptogam crust is broken and the grasses destroyed, it is very difficult, if not impossible, to restore them. Today there is so little undisturbed land remaining in the Oregon sage desert that it is challenging to even find an example of a true, healthy cryptogam crust or native bunch-grass prairie.

The story of the pronghorn antelope and other wildlife on the high desert begins and will end with native plants: Indian ricegrass, bluebunch wheatgrass, basin wild rye, low sagebrush, arrowleaf balsamroot, big sagebrush, Idaho fescue, bitterbrush, threadleaf sedge, spiny hopsage, and tapertip hawksbeard. Many of these plants were important to native peoples: Indian ricegrass for flour, sagebrush to cure cough and to construct clothing and shelter, arrowleaf balsamroot to cure stomach pains and headaches and for food. The native plants also provided excellent forage for larger animals like the antelope as well as cover and food for smaller animals and birds, but overgrazing and fire suppression broke up the cryptogam crust and disturbed the land, giving advantage to foreign annual plants and skewing the grass-to-shrub ratio in favor of the shrubs. With the cryptogams went the water-holding capacity of the desert crust, again to the detriment of the native grasses. Lack of periodic fires also aided the spread of shrubs, to the disadvantage of bunch grasses, which are not harmed by the fast-moving range fires.

Plant strategies have a great deal to do with what survives on the prairie. Foreign intruders such as cheatgrass put all of their energy into the annual production of seeds. (The best strategy on disturbed land is to grow quickly and produce lots of seeds.) The native perennials follow a different strategy because they must compete in the long term with other perennials. They develop relationships with the soil and cryptogams, put down three times as many roots as stems, collect as much water and nutrients as they can from soil symbionts, develop offensive smells and tastes to discourage predators, and recycle wastes to the soil. Some of these endemic plants even become drip irrigation systems by catching and more slowly releasing light rain and morning dew. And when a gully-washing thunderstorm comes along, the sudden flood of water is conserved by the cryptogam crust for later release to the extensive root system of the native perennials. Perennials produce far more abundant and higher-quality forage for wildlife than the temporary annuals that put most of their energy into making seeds to further propagate themselves.

The challenge on the refuge today is to reestablish native grasses. Managed use of range fire may help change the balance of nature in favor of the native grasses, as occurred when a large area of brush land in the refuge was burned in 1985 and subsequently reverted to grassland capable of providing better forage for antelope and other wildlife.

The pronghorn antelope is strictly a North American animal; it goes back in the fossil record twenty-five million years when at least thirteen

genera of antelope ranged the West. Only one genus survived the Pleistocene ice ages, making the antelope a remnant in eastern Oregon just like
the redband trout and the quaking aspen. The pronghorn is not a true
antelope, however, because it sheds its horns. True antelope, like gazelles
and wildebeests, do not shed their horns.

At the time of first European contact with the West, the antelope
population was perhaps forty to fifty million, but by the 1920s and 1930s
only about thirteen thousand remained in the entire West. In Oregon, the
population was in danger of complete elimination. President Franklin
Roosevelt was persuaded by regional advocates in 1935 to put aside the
prime antelope habitat of the Hart Mountain range by establishing the
Hart Mountain Antelope Refuge. Regulated grazing continued on the
refuge until just a few years ago when environmentalists obtained relief
in court to discontinue it. This was the first fault line in the rock-solid
ranching culture of Lake County in over one hundred years. The Hart
Mountain herd along with the Beaty Mountain herd now consists of about
fifty-two hundred animals.

The most remarkable attribute of the pronghorn, except for its legendary eyesight, is its incredible speed. Individual antelope have been
clocked at sixty miles per hour, and entire herds have been able to run at
forty miles per hour for ten minutes. Some pronghorn observers believe
that they are faster than a cheetah in a sprint of a half-mile or more. Recent finds of cheetah fossils in the Nevada desert suggest that antelope
are fast because of the cheetah. The pronghorn's keen eyesight and great
speed allow it to escape coyotes and mountain lions, but the young fawns
are vulnerable until they get their running legs. Then several interesting
body adaptations enable them to run fast: enlarged heart, lungs, and wind-
pipe compared to other animals of comparable size; nerveless padding
on the hooves; and dense leg bones with an additional layer of bone lami-
nate as compared to other animals.

Pronghorns were important to the material well-being of the northern
Paiute tribes who inhabited the Oregon desert. The tribes' means of hunting involved luring large numbers of antelope into circular sagebrush corrals by use of antelope disguises and mimicking antelope behaviors.
Drumming and singing were also used to "charm" the animals into ac-
ceptance of the slaughter. The circular brush corrals were up to two miles
around, remnants of which have been reported in the desert country of
northern Nevada. These methods were used particularly in winter when
the antelope ran in large herds, according to Isabel Kelly in her study on
Paiute culture.

My father observed that pronghorns were innately curious. On hiking trips in the desert, he would sometimes wave a white flag to attract them. Often our dog would give chase, but they would quickly tire him, leaving him disoriented and confused. We also noted impatient behavior by antelope. If our dog were near a water hole or spring they wanted to access, they would stand off and snort, trying to lure the dog away so they could circle back and drink.

The ultimate hope for the continued survival of the pronghorn lies in the restoration of the native grasses, but the hope is kindled by the hardiness and adaptability of the animal itself. This trait is well-illustrated by Arthur Einarsen, who studied the antelope at Hart Mountain for many years. He reported that when temperatures dropped to forty degrees below zero, the herds survived without fatalities, in apparent contentment. He also gave an eloquent statement of why the antelope should survive: "In body beauty, few animals equal the pronghorn antelope. The slender limbs and finely sculptured muscles combine the grace of Apollo and the speed of Mercury."

SIXTEEN

Redband

I will go to the desert today
and count the animals and plants
and air tides.
I will catalog my memories
and search for a place
to store them.
I will build a pool near the
stream to protect all that swim.

S OON AFTER I WAS old enough to walk, my father took me to his favorite high-desert streams to learn to fish. Fly fishing then was not the
expensive, elite sport it is now, but my father refused to use earthworms
to catch fish except out of desperation because he did not like to go home
empty-handed. I can only remember using worms in the early spring when
the creeks were running high and muddy. My father's fly-fishing equipment consisted of a simple reel that clicked, an old bamboo rod, a fly line,
a wicker basket filled with fresh wet grass, some leader, and a selection
of three fly patterns: mosquito, gray hackle yellow, and royal coachman.

My first rod was a willow branch with no reel, but later in life I would
graduate to fiberglass and then to graphite rods. My father sometimes used
waders, but generally we waded the streams in our normal leather working
boots because the waders invariably got cut when climbing barbed wire
fences. He taught me to avoid rattlesnake bites by never placing my hands
where I could not clearly see, to cast and bounce flies off rocks so they
would just kiss the water and drift down the riffles like real flies, to cast
under a cut bank, to avoid hanging up in the brush near the stream, and

to wait to fish until the direct sun was off the water. On the narrow, desert streams we fished, hanging up in the brush was the most serious problem; I soon learned to cast with little back cast, or better yet, to roll the cast into a hole sideways with no back cast at all.

Our favorite fishing spots were Deep Creek Canyon and Drakes Creek Canyon, both roadless and in the Warner Lakes drainage. We also fished Thomas Creek in the Goose Lake drainage and the Chewaucan River. The trip into Drakes Creek took the most effort because it required crossing a rocky sage flat followed by a steep descent down a rim rock face to the tiny stream. It was easy to get distracted by antelope viewing, wildflower observation, and deer spotting. Both canyons contained springs and aspen groves and even a few large, lonesome Ponderosa pines; the trees provided a nice spot for a nap while waiting for the direct sun to leave the water.

Our efforts were always rewarded with abundant strikes, plenty of fish to clean and eat at streamside and some left over to take home. My father invariably won the bet as to who would catch the first and largest fish. Preparation of fish proceeded by a set ritual. A small sagebrush or bark fire was made, and when it had burned down to coals, the trout were wrapped headless and clean into an aluminum foil pouch full of potatoes and wild onions collected streamside. After roasting in the coals, the baked fish were deboned with a single, deft tug along the backbone and the bright orange meat and skin eaten by hand. My father had an uncanny ability to judge the coals and pull the trout out just when they approached the best balance of juicy flavor and crispness.

There are two types of trout in the desert streams: planters and natives. The natives were of two types: small stream residents and the much larger spawners that came up from the Warner Lakes each spring to spawn in the shallow gravel. The hatchery planters were rainbow trout, eastern brook trout, or German brown trout. The natives—redband trout—were much more vigorous, colorful, cagey, and better to eat— always more active when hooked, more likely to dart from behind a rock or cut bank and strike like lightning, only to dive immediately under a rock or branch to try to tangle the line. In this they were often successful. Only the large lake trout spawners were sluggish: the males full of white foam and the females gorged with eggs that spurted out when touched. Today redband populations in the Oregon desert are proposed for listing under the Endangered Species Act, including those of the Warner Lakes, Goose Lake, and Chewaucan subspecies.

The isolation of the redband trout in the small streams of the Oregon desert began at the end of the last Pleistocene ice age when the vast, deep lakes began to dry. Dr. Ken Currens, a fish geneticist, thinks the Oregon desert redband may have been isolated from coastal and other rainbow forms up to 120,000 years ago. Today, redband trout exist in only about ten percent of their historic habitat due to overfishing, cattle grazing, deforestation, intermixing with planted fish, and stream pollution. Over a period of thousands of years the hardy redband have adapted to a harsh environment of spring floods, summer heat, periodic drought, and natural predation, but they still require clean, shaded water.

Of all the problems, deforestation of the headwaters of the desert streams and cattle grazing have taken the greatest toll. For example, Deep Creek originates in the high reaches of the forested Warner Mountains. Excessive timber harvesting has increased the stream silt, smothering the fertilized eggs of the redband in the gravel beds where they are laid. The deforestation also causes higher spring runoff and erosion of banks since the trees and understory are not present to absorb the snow melt and spring rains and slowly release it during the summer season. Grazing in the lower desert stretches of the stream has impacted the trout since the cattle graze the stream bank vegetation, collapse the undercut banks, and break the spongy layers on the desert floor. The result is less shade, less fish cover, less plant mass to store and release the water slowly, higher water temperature, more silt, and water polluted with animal waste which the stream bank vegetation cannot adequately process and cleanse.

Stream bank restoration benefits not only the trout but also a host of wildlife including birds, mammals, insects, plants, and even cattle. The stream bank riparian zones are like a magnet in the desert; they are the edges, the ecotones where life can find water, food, and cover in a hostile climate. As the land managers attempt to change old practices by fencing the riparian zones, moving the cattle to graze away from streams, replanting the stream banks, ceasing the planting of hatchery fish, and requiring catch-and-release of fish, there is hope that the feisty and ancient redband can survive the latest challenge to its existence.

Could it be that a royal coachman drifting down the clean, sparkling, cool riffles of Deep Creek on a summer afternoon will ignite once again a flurry of darting silver flashes from beneath rocks and cut banks? Will the water seem to boil with circular ripples in the evening as hungry fish pluck insects from the surface? Will it be possible to become like a child again with a willow pole and a dry fly?

SEVENTEEN

Semaphore Grass

I believe a leaf of grass is no less
than the journey-work of the stars.
—Walt Whitman

OREGON SEMAPHORE GRASS was first discovered in northern Oregon in 1886, but a second location was found in 1936 in the high desert near Adel. *Pleuropogon oregonus* then disappeared from human awareness for over forty years before it was rediscovered, again near Adel, in June of 1979. During that time, the grass was thought to be extinct; today it is considered threatened with extinction.

Semaphore grass grows in the standing water and slow-moving sloughs of Mud Creek near the Highway 140 bridge. The plant grows in colonies near various other sedges and grasses. It is distinctive because of unusual "grasshopper antennae" awns and seed heads which stick straight out from the stem, resembling semaphore flags. Unlike most grasses in the desert, it grows in water. It is a perennial plant, two to three feet high, and it flowers in June and July just at the time Mud Creek is usually high and muddy with spring melt from the Warner Mountains. Because of its very limited wet habitat, it is susceptible to drought and to human activities such as cattle grazing.

It is not known how long semaphore grass has lived in Lake County. As an angiosperm it is a member of a phylum which contains some 230,000 species and appeared 150 million years ago, a relatively young phylum as plants go. Since its home in the Warner Mountains is part of the Great Basin, and the mountains were formed about 17 million years ago, semaphore grass, while young for a plant, is old compared to the human species.

The Nature Conservancy has leased ten acres of Mud Creek to protect the grass and to provide it habitat. Often the Conservancy and other environmental groups cite the potential usefulness of plants as a rationale for their protection. What medicines might be extracted and synthesized? Could the genetic material be used to improve other water-loving cereals such as rice to feed a growing human population? These are perhaps sufficient reasons, but allowing a species to survive because of its usefulness is to say that human needs are an *a priori* criterion for survival. Therefore, some conservationists argue that other species deserve or even have a right to life and habitat whether or not we like them or whether they are useful to us. After all, human behavior long ago nullified with altruism whatever validity could be found in Darwin's evolutionary dictum of survival of the fittest. Humans are capable of great sacrifice to protect the helpless, weak, and disabled, including those who have no possibility of contributing to the gene pool. We cannot argue that humans always act to pass on their individual genes in the great chain of being or that they invariably conform to survival of the strongest or the fittest. In our own being there are remnants of nature's love for species and indifference to the individual, but why is altruism extended to other species?

Perhaps the question hinges on how we understand God. At least since the Egyptian pharaohs, the Yahweh of the Old Testament, and the Greek Apollo, our conception of God reflects a human form. The God of the Old Testament did not come up through nature: the great, sloshing sac of primordial ooze or the sluggish water of the semaphore grass. The God of the Old Testament simply existed *a priori* and created nature with, of all things, words. Not a sea or an atmosphere or a star or a lake gave rise to creation; words did. It was a God of human form and image that sounded the words of creation. With this God on our side, it was just a matter of time before the value of the individual human personality reigned over the face of the earth with all of its attendant benefits of democracy, freedom, science, technology, art, property rights, and capitalism. With this God in charge only human sentiment can be relied upon to protect any non-human species.

Yet, from time to time the smelly, chaotic, fecund, and indifferent womb of nature shakes our technical certainty, the instruments go off the dial, the heavens open, the earth shakes, people die, the torrents of catastrophe break loose from the frames we nailed them in, and prayers and rituals are offered up while the primordial, pagan universe roars outside our shaking doors. There will forever be a tension between the raw chaos of nature and the defined, logical, and ordered scientific flowering of the human mind. The gods of nature care about species and are indifferent to the individual. Yet something in us is attracted to the unrestrained surge of nature. The diminutive and seemingly fragile semaphore grasses of the world throw out seeds from their watery wombs, and we are somehow compelled to fence out the cows until the grasses can reinherit the earth.

EIGHTEEN

The Animal Wars

And after will I send for many hunters,
and they shall hunt them from every
mountain, and from every hill, and out of the holes
of the rocks.
—Jeremiah 16:16

I WAS PROBABLY ABOUT TWELVE when the word came to our Boy Scout troop to make war on magpies in the Oregon desert. The reason for the campaign rested on the belief by our leaders that because the magpies ate the eggs and young of other more demure birds, it was time for a good deed to be done to correct the situation. Our job was to take to the field at the proper time of year, locate magpie nests, and destroy the eggs. Because magpies build extremely sturdy nests complete with roofs, branch framing, and clay-lined walls up in trees, this was easier said than done. Even though their nests are well-constructed, magpies usually use them only for a year or two. Other birds and animals often adopt the structures for their own nests. Given our lack of skill in egg identification, it is possible that we destroyed more eggs of birds we were trying to help than those of the magpies themselves. After a trip or two to the field, our commitment to the magpie war quickly waned, without much apparent damage to their population.

The magpie is not a well-loved bird despite its handsome appearance. The first recorded encounter with them occurred in 1804 by the Lewis and Clark expedition, and it did not go well. The magpies entered the tents and took meat from the dishes. The birds are also noisy and raucous, notorious scavengers, and general pests in the regard of many. They are not graceful fliers like hawks, eagles, gulls, or swallows; they are more creatures of the branch and ground. They are so aggressive that they are known to form associations with hawks, eagles, and even coyotes to scavenge the kills made by these hunters. Magpies also share the problem of eating the poison bait intended for the coyote. Yet magpies are not without redeeming social and family qualities; they are not entirely without friends. Observations indicate that magpies mate for life, the male feeds the female while on the nest, and the nest is kept very clean by removal of the fecal sacs of the young. Western songwriter and singer Ian Tyson likes magpies so much that he calls them coyotes of the sky; he even wrote a song for them.

Soon after the magpie mission our troop was enlisted for yet another search-and-destroy campaign: the porcupine war. For a time a bounty was even paid for each porcupine nose we brought in. Porcupines girdled pine and fir trees, thus depriving loggers of work and their families of food—or so the logic went. Later in my college years, I worked each summer for the Forest Service, and although I did see an occasional tree damaged by porcupines, it was clear that one logger in a single day could do more damage to a forest than all the porcupines in Lake County could do in a year. Porcupines did not prove easy to kill with the weapons we scouts had at our disposal. After a few experiences with the human-like sounds and cries for mercy the animal could make while being stoned and clubbed, we quickly retreated from warring on the porcupine population.

Our dogs learned the hard way about the hardiness of porcupines. Contrary to popular myth, a porcupine cannot throw its hollow, barbed quills, but it is very adept with its tail when attacked by a dog. When my favorite dog Mickey got a mouthful of quills on a fishing trip to Drakes Creek Canyon, my father, not willing to pay for a veterinarian, simply braced Mickey's mouth open with a stick and pulled the quills out one by one with pliers. My father's philosophy on many aspects of life was, "You need to graduate from the school of hard knocks." Luckily, Mickey survived the ordeal and did not attack porcupines again, but other dogs were not so fortunate.

Coyote wars were also waged in Lake County. To hunt coyotes, more sophisticated weapons were needed than those available to a scout troop, so we were not recruited to hunt them. We did worry about our dogs getting into the poison bait and traps left for the coyotes by the professional hunter the county employed. The coyote wars were particularly intense when the sheep industry in Lake County was in its heyday. In recent years, coyotes have adapted well to human encroachment, and they are back in large numbers. Recently, the U.S. Fish and Wildlife Service attributed a decline in the numbers of antelope fawns to the predation of coyotes. A special hunt was planned on the Hart Mountain Antelope Refuge, but the hunt was stopped by a court case brought by an environmental group. The environmentalists argued that it is best to leave the balance of nature up to nature. In the past when humans have intervened on behalf of or opposed to some animal or another, the balance has been disrupted, leading to new problems or exacerbation of existing problems. The coyote has some friends, and they may yet prevail.

The coyote has held an interesting place in the mythology of Native American tribes including the northern Paiute who inhabited Lake County. The coyote was often viewed as a greedy and licentious trickster, but the coyote secured fire and pine nuts, gave mankind arts and crafts, released game, and created the earth from the world ocean along with the even more powerful wolf deity. Mankind was created when coyote had sexual relations with two women. He also ordered death to occur among mankind, something akin to God ordering death after the Adam and Eve incident in the garden of paradise. Coyote figures in so many stories, songs, and myths among various tribes as a transformer and trickster that it is difficult to summarize them all. To this day the coyote remains a quintessential icon in the cowboy mythology of the West as well: a symbol of lonely, romantic independence and freedom. Even western music adopts, transforms, and abstracts the coyote's lilting howl into the high-pitched, yodel-like refrains of ballads.

Of all the animal wars in Lake County, I most vividly remember the war on mule deer. During the 1940s and 1950s, there was a superabundance of mule deer. Hunting them was an important rite of passage for any young man old enough to carry a rifle. It was common practice to skip school in the fall during the opening days of deer season. Some school districts for a time gave up and simply closed school on the opening day. The mark of manhood was to kill at least a four-point: a buck with four points on its antlers on each side. It was not good form to kill a "spike": a yearling buck with only one point on each side of the antlers. To kill a doe, even by accident, was beneath contempt. The successful hunter would show off the kill by driving through town with the dead deer strapped to the hood or fenders of the vehicle used in the hunt—usually a pickup truck. Sometimes the head and antlers would be displayed by being tied to the roof of the vehicle. After World War II, when the lumber-based economy of Lake County went into recession and the mill workers were unemployed for a time, it was common practice to kill an illegal buck or

The author (far left) on a mule deer hunting trip with his father (far right). *(Photo from the author's collection)*

two to feed the family during the winter. The game warden, a friend to most of the people in the town, would look the other way if the crime was not too obvious or egregious.

Sometime in the late 1950s the culture began to change. The state game commission of Oregon became convinced that the sage, bitterbrush, and grassland range of the deer could not support the population. They believed that too many deer were starving in the winter due to inadequate forage. For a time, hunters were given packets of bitterbrush seed to plant in the field to attempt to improve the food source. The commission conducted show-and-tell trips to the winter ranges to show the extent of the problem. I remember such a trip with my father to the border region of California near the south end of Goose Lake. The game biologists took us to the sage and grass flats where deer accumulated during the winter to escape the deep snows of the Warner Mountains. I had often been astonished by the size of deer herds we would see in the wild, but this trip staggered the imagination. Thousands of deer stood in hundreds of herds across mile after mile of range. It was not long afterward that doe seasons were opened and hunting became an extremely regulated and controlled activity. The large herds were soon gone, and with them went the rites and mythology of the hunt so prevalent in our town. Hunting today is a legalistic, high-tech sport for those lucky enough to get deer, antelope, elk, or mountain sheep tags and affluent enough to buy the equipment.

Today my shotgun and deer rifle sit unused in a closet. They are aging but clean; I do not even own shells for them. I keep them as a symbol and reminder of the blood of the animals that were killed. I seek some redemption by visiting the range lands of Lake County with only a camera. I do not know what my daughters will think of the guns or do with them when I am gone.

NINETEEN

The Lost Forest

Beneath this cathedral of sky,
beneath this parquetry of sage,
piles of diatoms,
glassy window cells,
remember the Pleistocene light,
the rising and falling ice,
the morning after glacial night.

THE SECOND TIME I traveled to the Lost Forest, I went alone. I went to understand desolation: of a place and of its soul. The Lost Forest defines the geography of desolation; it is the compass center of emptiness.

To the north of the Lost Forest, plates of rock shear—a band of faults, the Brother's Fault Zone, slashes across Oregon, ending at the Newberry Crater near Bend.

To the southeast of the Lost Forest lies Alkali Lake; its cracked, white moods shift in sunlight and wind. A small spring and pool spreads and sinks into the dry flat that is the lake. In the pool, a tiny fish, the Hutton Spring tui chub, clings to an anachronistic existence, marooned on a dry sea of salt. Nowhere else on the planet does this fish live. Although scientists think it gained access to the Alkali Lake Basin some forty-six thousand years ago, this species has yet to be given a Latin name or described by science. Hutton Spring is an old stagecoach stop, but the road has faded. Nearby, a toxic waste dump lies marked and buried on a greasewood flat, too isolated for the state of Oregon to worry much about cleaning it up.

To the south of the Lost Forest at Fossil Lake, the wind tears bones out of the cracked earth: two-million-year-old mammoths, camels, flamingos, pelicans, salmon, and mineralized sloth. Their fragments hint at a lost, wet paradise.

To the west of the Lost Forest, volcanic geometries erupt in the lyric, jagged language of geology: tufts and cinder cones, air-falls, cinder bombs, breccia, agglutinated eruptive splatter, mafic vents, silicic domes, scoriaceous cinders, fissure eruptions. The sounds roll off the tongue in angular hissing sounds as if blown from a molten crater. The map of the area recites a litany of names, a descriptive topography: Crack-in-the-Ground, Big Hole, Fort Rock, Devil's Garden, Hole-in-the-Ground.

To the southwest of the Lost Forest, lakes once teemed with tiny glass cells called diatoms, beautifully etched in microscopic profusion, full of green and golden chlorophyll, concentrating the sun in the waters. As the lakes dried, foot after foot, ton after ton of diatoms piled up, squeezed into diatomaceous earth. Today the earth is exhumed to make household products, from cat litter to cleansers, for filtration and as filler.

At the immediate boundary of the Lost Forest, giant dunes encroach: remnants of drying lakes and failed homesteads that opened the land to the wind. White, bare skeletons of dead junipers suffocate in the sand. But some live, etched and sculptured, exuding time, character, and toxins to keep other plants from growing underneath them and stealing their water.

At the forest center, ponderosa pines grow in half the needed rain; the porous sand quickly absorbs what falls, removes it from the reach of dry wind and hot sun. Clay soils beneath the sand perch the water in root zones. Great gnarled junipers and yellow-barked pines stand dependent on a fortunate layering of sand and clay. Six communities of plants tenaciously cling frozen in time, the past scattered around them: the juniper/fescue community, the ponderosa pine/big sagebrush community, the ponderosa pine/bitterbrush community, the pine/juniper/sagebrush community, the big sagebrush community, and the silver sagebrush community. Beneath the brush I find the rare green-tinged paintbrush in bloom on a sand pile.

An interminable wind sifts through the Lost Forest, reminding it of an outside world. The forest sighs in the wind, the past scattered around it in volcanic geometry, planes of alkali, diatomaceous piles, hills of sand, and bone fragments. The Lost Forest waits for the millennium of the return of the lakes.

PART FOUR

NATIVES

TWENTY

Goose Lake

Not a single bird
among thousands falls,
the city does not fall,
nor the rain,
nothing quite touches
the earth.

I AM FASCINATED WITH Goose Lake: the squall lines that move across it and hide it in snow in the winter, the virga not quite touching it in summer, the sparkling waves of moonlight reflecting from it on autumn evenings. It is possible to believe that the world was created from such waters.

My most profound experience with it occurred in a grain field near the lake one cold winter morning at dawn. I was about sixteen and often went hunting alone on weekend mornings during season. I had set up goose decoys, made a blind, and settled under a white sheet to blend in with the snow on the field. It was important to be ready before dawn, since the ducks flew at first light with the geese following after the sun was up. It was a blustery winter day, not the best for hunting. I could hear a few flocks of early ducks overhead in the dark, moving north to the Summer Lake basin, their wings whistling in the darkness. I tried to keep my hands from freezing to the metal of the long barrel of my single-shot 20-gauge, an ancient firearm even then. As soon as the sun came up, clouds of geese, ducks, and cranes began to rise from Goose Lake. Flock after flock flew overhead in stacked layers; the racket soon was louder than the wind. Some of the flocks broke from the northward procession to circle, set wings, and land in the decoys right in front of me. I fired and reloaded a few times, but the geese continued to land in total indifference while the dark main cloud of birds continued to pass by above them. The procession went on for over an hour. There were flocks of geese extending from the town of Lakeview several miles to the east and across the horizon to the west side of the valley, itself many miles distant. It must have been a scene like Audubon witnessed before the passenger pigeons became extinct. After a few shots, I dropped the gun and just stood up; there was no need for a blind. It was the beginning of the end of my interest in hunting.

Goose Lake was once a cultural intersection: a place of abundant game and waterfowl, where swarms of native trout spawned in the small streams feeding the lake. Four tribes used portions of the lake valley in various cycles throughout the year: the Klamaths, the Modocs, the Achomawi, and the northern Paiute. The tribes left evidence of their presence in artifacts, arrowheads, and petroglyphs. A portion of the valley, such as Sugar Hill, named by Europeans who spilled sugar from a wagon, was sacred to the Achomawi, who did not camp near it or even approach it.

Goose Lake was also an important intersection for the early pioneers arriving on the Applegate Trail. After crossing long stretches of desert and climbing the steep east side of the Warner Mountains through Fandango Pass, the lake became visible below. It seemed an incredible oasis to many of the argonauts when they first saw it, particularly after the climb from the desert which required up to twelve oxen per wagon. It is said that some celebrated and danced, giving the Fandango Pass its name from the Spanish word, although others maintain that the pass was named for a tragic Indian attack and raid on a wagon train. Still another story claims that a train camping at the pass encountered a storm so bad that the men had to dance to keep warm. Whatever the origin of the name, the viewpoint of pioneer P.F. Castleman, who stood in the pass in September of 1849, is revealing:

> We could see Goose Lake which was several miles distant in the west. It was now near sunset and there were a great many trains encamped near the margin of this valley and as the peaceful smoke seemed to rise and hover over the valley which was covered with cattle and horses I thought it was the grandest scene I had ever seen.

After the descent from Fandango Pass to the lake, a number of wagon trains dissolved, based on decisions to continue south to the gold fields of California via the Lassen Trail or whether to continue west on the Applegate Trail to the Rouge River and Willamette valleys. The lure of California was expressed by the words of a folk song at the time. "Oh, California! / Thou land of glittering dreams, / Where the yellow dust and diamonds, boys, / Are found in all thy streams!"

Since my morning with the geese at Goose Lake, I often wonder what a native hunter saw as he floated in a tule raft on the lake or hunkered behind a brush or rock blind near its edge. He hunted using small arrow points or nets. His duck decoys made of tule have been found and relegated to our museums. The flocks must have been so great that he might have imagined every star fading in the morning sky to become birds inhabiting the air of Goose Lake. Did his thoughts lean to astonishment as did mine that winter morning?

My mind returns to childhood when a friend of my father went out alone on a boat at night on Goose Lake. The next morning we joined the search along the shores near Pine Creek. He was never found. I like to think he was lured to the water of the lake—seduced by moonlight sparkling on the waves.

On my morning of epiphany in the grain fields near Goose Lake, the wild geese were calling over the tule margins and glittering ripples. The calls repeated over and over the stories and memories when the geese first arose and flew from the primordial waters of creation. On these waters I too will be scattered.

TWENTY-ONE

The Achomawi

In the desert night,
in the fullness of memory,
the coyote
chants to the moon,
it is the closing hour,
nothing is lost.

FIRST SAW THEM in a picture made about 1910 somewhere near Goose Lake. There are twelve of them on horses. The one in the middle, probably the leader, has a hand raised to the sky, palm outward, in a gesture of greeting. Several of the men wear head dresses of feathers while antelope horns adorn another, probably a shaman. The women wear blankets around their shoulders, scarves over their heads, and beads. One of the women, ahead of the rest, also stands out because of her white horse. Perhaps she is the wife of the leader or the leader herself. It is a picture of remnants of a proud culture which lived in a beautiful place for thousands of years before Christ, before the printing press, before the wheel, before even the bow and arrow.

They had probably lived on the land for ten thousand years. There were never more than three thousand of them altogether in the tribe, which was scattered in small bands over a large area of what is now northeastern California and southeastern Oregon. They were the Achomawi or Pit River tribe, but some of them frequented the shores of Goose Lake.

They believed that the world was made by a silver fox thinking about a clump of sod, and fox sang while he held the clump of sod. He and coyote threw the clump of sod down from the clouds and by singing and dancing stretched it out and made mountains, valleys, trees, and rocks. The

Achomawi thought that everything was alive, even rocks, and that the shaman could travel to other worlds through circles pecked on the rocks.

The Achomawi also knew about "dinihowi"—luck in gambling, love, and hunting. They went to the mountains to find luck. They would become tired and scared, cry, go hungry for days. While in this state they would attract the pity of an animal and be taught its song. The animal could be a wolf, a blue jay, or even a fly. They would remember the song and when they needed help return to the sacred spot and sing the song, and the animal spirit would return. Some natives would obtain "damaagome"—more mean and quarrelsome than the peaceful "dinihowi"—and would possess the medicine to be a shaman.

Those who became shamans faced a more dangerous life, and none were anxious for this. They were required to suck their patients in the regions of disease to remove the poisoning sometimes placed by other shamans. They were also in danger of losing their souls. Departing souls of the dead, not wanting to travel alone, would induce others to follow, and the shaman was called upon to bring back souls enticed to such travel. Since no one wanted to give a departed soul a reason to return, the names of the dead were taboo, and the dead were cremated and everything belonging to them burned.

The lives of the Achomawi were suffused with stories and spirits. The old stories were told during winter nights as small bands huddled in the partially subterranean, tule-covered lodges for warmth. To them there was no apparent difference or division between religious feeling and earth, or between nature and spirit, or between story and place. Over forty sacred places were located and named, and art was pecked onto the rocks at some of these places by shamans. Entire mountains such as Sugar Hill on the southeast shore of Goose Lake were deemed sacred.

The Hewisedawi group of Achomawi lived on the north fork of the Pit River and on Goose Lake. They dug pits along the river to catch deer, hence their European name. They caught Goose Lake redband trout and the Goose Lake sucker: large landlocked species with no outlet to the sea. Numerous streams including the Pit River were used to harvest salmon, bass, trout, and mussels. Rock corrals were built in the streams to spear and net the fish. They hunted deer, antelope, and mountain sheep in the Warner Mountains, the faulted rims to the east of Goose Lake. They made bows of yew and juniper, gathered abundant wild plums, camas bulbs, and seeds from many plants. Sage hen, rabbits, beaver, bears, deer, squirrel, otter, wolves, and mountain lions were plentiful; in the spring and fall, Goose Lake teemed with thousands of geese and ducks. Plant fibers were used to make baskets and nets. When rain was needed, holes were pecked in sacred rocks by the rain shaman. When the Hewisedawi were unaware, the more aggressive Modocs to the north and west would raid and take them for slaves to be traded as far north as the Dalles on the Columbia River.

By 1936, due to disease, poverty, and cultural disintegration, about five hundred Achomawi were left. None live on Goose Lake or near the sacred Sugar Hill. The flocks of geese and ducks are a mere remnant of their former number. The Goose Lake sucker, redband trout, and tui chub are rare and in danger in the lake's waters, yet the Goose Lake Valley and the Warner Mountains retain a raw, primitive beauty.

The Achomawi called the European invaders "inillaaduwi" (tramps). They said about them, "They do not believe anything is alive. They are dead themselves." On crystal fall days when the wild plums are sweet, and the winds in the canyons of the Warner Mountains carry a hint of the cold weather to come, and you can see a hundred miles across the desert, and the aspen leaves are changing color in the high air, it is possible to believe in redemption for ourselves and for the land. It is necessary to invest in the land some measure of spirit and to sanctify it as did the Achomawi.

TWENTY-TWO

The Groundhog Eaters

In flurries,
in feathers,
in stones,
you are here.

T HEY WERE A BAND of northern Paiutes known as Gidutikad—groundhog eaters. They lived in Warner Valley, and we know a great deal
about them thanks to the work of Isabel Kelly and her ethnological studies.
Sometimes they crossed the Warner Mountains over Fandango Pass to
hunt on the eastern shore of Goose Lake. They named the pass Paduaagan
from the word for grizzly bear. They wintered in the Warner Valley near
the village of Plush where Honey Creek entered the valley (Sagana-
matsibui) or near the village of Adel where Deep Creek entered (Saib).
(The village of Plush was named for a local Paiute who got into a crooked
poker game and mispronounced the word "flush" by saying "plush"; he
and the town were named such ever since.)

The Gidutikad captured deer in pitfalls, charmed antelope into brush
corrals two miles around, killed grizzly bear, drove rabbits into nets by
communal drives, hunted ducks with tule decoys from brush blinds, took
geese from tule rafts (balsa), ate bird eggs of all types, gathered ripe wild
plums in the fall from the slopes of the Warner Mountains, scooped fish
from the streams using sagebrush baskets, gathered seeds of many types
and dug roots of camas in the Big Valley, dressed wounds with sagebrush
extract, treated burns with the powder of burned cattail pods, and used
an infusion of the crushed leaves of rabbit brush for bad colds. The high
meadows, sage flats, alkali bottoms, and lake shores were their apothecary.

Their winter houses were conical lodges covered with tule or sage mats. They wore shirts of sagebrush bark or buckskin, blankets of rabbit skin and sagebrush leggings and moccasins. Willow was used for burden baskets, winnowing, seed beating, fish traps, water jars, spoons, and cups. They made cradles, snowshoes, musical instruments, tools, and weapons from what they could find locally from the earth or trade with nearby tribes. Their bows were made of juniper, the arrows of rose currant, and the strings of deer sinew; the glue came from the Warner sucker.

In stories they taught that stone items were made when animals were people; the pestle was left near water by the cannibalistic being Numuzoho, who was driven into the lake. The cannibalistic being Bahizoho, who was an animal that looked like a man, created the mortars. The petroglyphs were made by Numuna, the people's father.

Dead people returned to look for their possessions before leaving for the abode of the dead in the Milky Way, so care was taken to burn these possessions lest the dead disturb the living. The stars of the Big Dipper were their people driving rabbits into nets. They forecast the weather with omens and used the bull roarer to influence the weather and melt the snow. For amusement they danced and played a variety of games; they loved gambling. They traded with the Achomawi but drove the Klamaths from the Warner Valley to the west of Goose Lake.

They lived in the land of the groundhog eaters for thousands of years, but they obtained the horse late compared to other tribes, perhaps only one hundred to two hundred years before white contact. By the time they met General Crook on the field of battle, they used the horse effectively and put up a good fight for their numbers, in small mounted bands or as individuals alone.

Chief Lakeview photographed at Lakeview, date unknown.
(Photo courtesy of the Lake County Historical Society)

PART FIVE

IMMIGRANTS

TWENTY-THREE

Death of an Explorer

*I imagine the forever
of ice and wind,
the endless wetting
and drying of the soul.
Can a speck
of consciousness
survive this elemental
harshness?*

I T IS INTRIGUING how the lives of people in the past intersect with our own in often unexpected ways. I grew up in a town at the foot of the Warner Mountains, hunted in the Warner Lakes, and even pursued Warner's profession of surveyor, but it took thirty-five years after my final summer in the mountains named for him before I had the slightest curiosity about the man himself. Since virtually nothing is known about Captain Warner before he entered West Point in 1831, I can understand him only by understanding my own experience as surveyor and knowledge of the mountains that bear his name and his lost remains.

The Warner Mountains are a north-south bearing fault block range so typical of the long ranges in the great Basin and Range of the American West, but the Warner Range is distinct from the other great alignments because of its overlay of a unique human history. To imagine the range it is first necessary to understand the thin atmosphere above it, which offers little obstruction to crystal clarity, and the light which changes constantly, painting the range white and silver in winter, soft green in early spring fading to yellow, gold, and saturated orange through summer and fall. The cycles of color change not only seasonally, but daily as well; the times just before and after sunrise are bathed in mystical blues, blacks, and deep violets, whereas at sunset the barren rock rims become bright neon purples, reds, and oranges. I have been to no other place where color claims the imagination so much as it does in the Warner Mountains.

In my college years, I returned to the Warners each summer to survey roads for the Forest Service. The pay was good for a college student, and there were no distractions to claim wages other than a necessary trip to town to buy groceries each week or so. We camped in tents at Can Spring in the Warner Range, never bathed or shaved, wore filthy clothes, never read or listened to any news, and were generally uncivilized; we probably resembled Captain Warner's party on his first and last sojourn into the range. The work was physically demanding but great fun because we were always beyond the end-of-the-road where untouched springs, aspen groves, old Ponderosa pine stands, beaver dams, wildflower fields, deer and antelope herds, coyotes, and cougars offered themselves to our amazement, entertainment, and astonishment. We seldom saw anyone beyond our own group, the only evidence of past human visitation being an occasional aspen bark carving left by a sheepherder. Even the foreign exchange students invariably on our crew, the city boys who signed up for a summer's work, and the occasional Forest Service engineer visiting from town were taken with the range. They often said, "This is beautiful," lacking a more expressive vocabulary to portray what was all around them. Little did I know at the time that our camp at Can Spring was just a mile or so from another namesake for Captain Warner: new Fort Warner. The fort was founded by General Crook during his campaigns in the region; today barely a trace of it remains.

It was near Can Spring that I first realized that trees were not just alive but had souls. This knowledge came to me inescapably and absolutely one morning in a Ponderosa pine grove near our camp. The sunlight of morning activated the east-facing bark of a giant pine, and the bark began to glow with a vibrant red and orange. The tree and then the whole grove seemed activated, charged with some ethereal internal energy for which the sunlight was only a catalyst. I felt the overwhelming presence of empathy as if the trees somehow cared for me, were praying for me because I was so temporary, fragile; because my metabolism was so fast that I missed the essence of light, wind, snow, and time. They watched mountains dissolve, felt in their roots what I could only understand as an abstract idea. Much later in life, in an aspen grove near Can Spring, a similar experience occurred. The aspen bark began to glow white in the light and thousands of leaves rattled in a breeze; I had the certain feeling that the aspen grove was a collection of departed souls reincarnated in communal roots, the phloem and xylem of complete families and tribes. It was as if lost souls had found a home in the aspen colony, much as the Native Americans of the region believed that departed souls become stars in the Milky Way. I have never experienced these feelings in any church, but when I take part in the mass, I am invariably reminded of the trees in the Warner Range.

Prior to my Forest Service years, my father and I hunted, fished, and collected rocks and memories in the mountains so visible right outside our window. In the fall we gathered the ripe wild plums, the same fruit that sustained the natives and later the pioneers and settlers. To this day, I return to the Warner Range each fall to taste the wild plums; it is a necessary sacrament, a way to remember my mother who loved them. I still have not relocated the logs of petrified wood that I found as a child on a plum-hunting expedition with my father so many years ago, but I vividly remember being separated from him for a time and finding log after log of rock scattered about the slope overlooking Goose Lake. No doubt this site was one of the sources of petrified wood and agate we collected by the bucketful in the dry washes of the valley below.

Captain Warner came to this region in the early fall of 1849, his orders to find a railroad route from the headwaters of the Sacramento River across the Sierra Nevada to the Humboldt River. When he arrived at his namesake range, he was far from the Humboldt and was not in the Sierra Nevada nor at the headwaters of the Sacramento. He was lost. In fact, his expedition was ill-fated from the beginning. He did not leave Sacramento until August, thereby placing the expedition in a race to avoid early snows in the mountains. His military escort was unwieldy and soon dropped out in a "hospital camp," sick with fever. His party began to meet half-starved forty-niners who had split from the Applegate Trail at Goose Lake to head south to the gold fields of California. The forty-niners depleted his supplies, but he did hire a few of them to replace his sick soldiers—although most of the forty-niners were in poor condition themselves. When Warner reached Lassen's Pass where the Applegate Trail crossed the range that would be named for him, he realized that the pass was unsuitable for a railroad. Leaving a Lieutenant Williamson in charge of a camp on Goose Lake, Warner proceeded north along the western front of the range with a group of only nine men, including the former Hudson's Bay Company guide and trapper François Bercier. Seventy miles north he finally outdistanced the range after passing Abert Rim and Lake Abert and came to what today is called the hogback: a pass to the east suitable for the construction of a railroad. Of course, a railroad was never built on the hogback because by this time Warner was far north of the Humboldt River and the Sierra Nevada range.

Warner and his small group passed over the hogback to the east and commenced south along the eastern face of the range. Somewhere on a stream near the current Oregon-California border, on September 26, 1849, the men were ambushed by natives. Warner was reportedly killed by "eleven" arrows, Bercier by "nine," and civilians George Cave and Henry Barling were also hit. Cave died on the way to Sacramento, but Barling would recover. It is a mystery how this party under fire from "twenty-five" hostiles had time to count arrows and Indians but no time to remove Warner's body. A Captain Lyon was ordered to the site a year later, but only evidence of a fire pit with some bone fragments was found. Either Warner was cremated by the assailants or, more likely, his mule was cooked for a feast. His body, bones, and personal effects have never been found. His assistant in the United States Topographical Engineers, Lieutenant Williamson, would prepare a map in 1866 that would for the first time name the range "Warner's Range" and for the first time correctly dissociate the range from the Sierra Nevada.

It is likely that Warner's life intersected with my ancestors before he met his fate in the Warner Mountains. After graduating from West Point, he took part in the forced Cherokee emigration known as the "Trail of Tears," wherein five civilized tribes were compelled to move from their ancestral homes in the Southeast to the Oklahoma and Arkansas territory to the west. My great grandfather Cheatham on my mother's side was Arkansas Cherokee. My grandfather Hudson clearly reveals his Cherokee heritage in the faded pictures I have of him: high cheekbones, coal black hair, and dark skin. Perhaps it is an ironic justice that Captain Warner perished at the hands of "uncivilized" native peoples after his participation in the bloody removal of the civilized tribes from their ancestral homelands.

I like to think that Captain Warner has redeemed himself, that his spirit has taken up residence in an aspen grove in the Warner Mountains, that he will live forever in the range named for him, and that he will cause us to remember the range as it was, as he saw it before it was logged, mined, and grazed. When the Ponderosa pine bark glows in morning light and the aspen leaves give voice to the mountain breezes, I imagine that one of the voices is his.

TWENTY-FOUR

Starved Out

Upon this aspen bark,
upon this cambric skin,
the book of pioneers
closes,
signatures fold in pages
of leaf and time.

A S SETTLERS BOUND FOR the Willamette Valley sought to avoid the treacherous trip down the gorge of the Columbia River, a few attempted to cross the grasslands, sage desert, and alkali flats of eastern Oregon. The results were sometimes disastrous. Wagontire Mountain in northern Lake County takes its name from an abandoned wagon wheel found there, the result of an Indian attack on settlers, at least according to one version of the origin of the name.

According to Bill Brown's biographer Edward Gray, it was not long after the first wagons traversed the desert of north Lake County that Brown began to build a legendary horse empire on the open range of eastern Oregon. In actuality, the empire began with sheep. In the summer of 1882, Bill Brown and his two brothers drove fifteen hundred sheep from the Willamette Valley over the Cascades to Wagontire Mountain and the Sinks of Lost Creek. (This example of back migration to the east, bucking the general flow of human movement to the west, is typical of the settlement and habitation of eastern Oregon, which occurred relatively late in the settlement of the West. To the initial streams of Oregon-bound settlers, eastern Oregon was viewed as an obstacle and a wasteland rather than an opportunity.) The first setback for the brothers occurred in the winter of

1884–85 when deep snow, a thaw, and then severe cold created a thick crust of frozen snow. Because most of the sheep were unable to paw through it for forage, their herd of five thousand was reduced to seven hundred. This type of disaster was common on the Oregon high desert. Nonetheless, by 1920 the sheep herd numbered about forty thousand.

Bill Brown also began rounding up wild horses and breeding them with Shires from England and Percherons from France. By 1918 horses with his Horseshoe Bar brand ranged from Fort Rock to Wagontire to Alkali Lake. Brown owned the largest branded horse herd in the Pacific Northwest. His animals combined strengths of the native and immigrant breeds and, because they could maneuver at fast gaits, became a favorite with armies. At auctions he sold his horses five hundred at a time; they fought for the United States in the war with Spain in Cuba and the Philippines, with the English in the Boer War, and with the allies in World War I. The Lake County horses were alleged to have more strength, wind, and endurance than those from more humid climates; it was said they could be ridden fifty to one hundred miles a day or pull a wagon fifty to sixty miles a day.

Brown's territorial strategy was to claim and control water sources, including all of those on the west side of Wagontire Mountain, thus guaranteeing his herds sole access to a vast grazing area. His domain read like a gazetteer of northern Lake County water sources: Benjamin Lake, Bradley Meadows, Chicago Valley, Edes Well, Goodrich Well, Hayes Spring, Langdon Spring, Lost Creek Spring, Perry Place, Sand Springs, and the Sinks of Lost Creek.

Brown's control over this land empire was not without challenges. In 1886 Brown killed John Overstreet in a gunfight over a land dispute, though Brown was never jailed or sent to trial. His horses were also the target of rustlers who used a two-hundred-acre meadow in the East Lava Beds to hide the stolen stock. The hideout, called "Robber's Roost," featured a narrow trail only six feet wide and eight feet high to reach a large meadow concealed on all sides by lava rock. It was the kind of hideout that is every kid's fantasy. Only after a certain "Singing Bill" gave information to the law was the Roost uncovered. Singing Bill disappeared thereafter, and his body was never discovered.

Bill Brown was known as a generous and decent man, keeping his relatively well-paid hands employed during the 1920s and 1930s after the market for horses and sheep softened. Eventually the Great Depression, the rustlers, the weather, the livestock markets, his basic charity, and the land itself conspired to end the empire. He died relatively poor in the Methodist Old People's Home in Salem, Oregon: a supreme irony that a man of the Oregon desert—a man who had seen his share of tough times, bad weather, and violence—should meet his end on the humid west side with his boots off.

By 1905 another human enterprise was under way on the high desert of northern Lake County, and, for a time, it appeared that the desolate region would remain permanently settled. In response to the Homestead Act and the prospect of free land, shopkeepers, schoolteachers, tradesmen, farmers, and many others mostly from the east—few with any experience of the desert or its climate—arrived to claim acreage and establish farms. They arrived during a series of mild, wet years, prompted by the myth held throughout the West that the rain would follow the plow, meaning that the ground once plowed would somehow encourage more rain. Towns were incorporated, post offices opened, schools and churches built, and ice cream socials held at the lava tube ice caves in the heat of summer. A weekly stage service from Silver Lake carried passengers and mail to Arrow, Viewpoint, Sink, Connley, Fleetwood, Loma Vista, Woodrow, Burleson, and Wastina, but by the early 1920s the desert had starved out most of the settlers; hoards of rabbits, lack of rain and irrigation, blowing sand, short growing seasons, and extremes of weather prevailed to expel them. Most headed west to the burgeoning sawmill town of Bend to find employment. They left behind a land opened and exposed to the wind, resulting in a dune field larger than any found on the Oregon coast. The dunes to this day encroach on the juniper and pine remnants found in the Lost Forest. The homestead era had lasted only fifteen years.

By the onset of World War II, little human activity remained in north Lake County except for some traditional cattle grazing, but the region again attracted attention. Army officers found the isolated expanse of land they needed to train soldiers for the coming desert battles of North Africa. By the summer of 1943, the population of the Oregon desert exploded to fifty thousand; an airfield and communication lines were built, tanks maneuvered, and the abandoned farmhouses of the homesteaders used for target practice. The desert responded with one of the worst dust storms ever recorded in the region; once again the land foiled human enterprise with its own untamed intentions. When the mock battles were over, the men went to the real war in Europe, and the Oregon desert returned to its own silent purposes.

There are today new signs of human enterprise on the high desert of north Lake County: deep wells irrigate alfalfa fields, a small plant processes diatomaceous earth for cat litter boxes, a very expensive over-the-horizon radar station stands mostly unmanned in mute deference to the end of the cold war. Near Alkali Lake, where Bill Brown ran his horses, a toxic waste dump lies largely forgotten save for a few drums emerging in the wind and blowing alkali dust. Nearby in a small fenced pond at Hutton spring, the old stagecoach stop, the Hutton tui chub clings to a precarious existence surrounded by alkali flats and wind. The tiny bodies of bone, scale, and fin of this delicate fish may yet outlast the dreams, empires, and armies of humankind. They wait in patience for the return of the deep lakes and the baptismal cleansing of the last vestige of the human presence.

Remnants of the Shirk cattle empire near Guano Lake. *(Melvin Adams)*

TWENTY-FIVE

Shirk Ranch

And in the end,
the thought of you
remained
ready for the spring.

I T APPEARS a lost wooden vessel on a great sea of sage and bunch grass; it is two stories with ship lap siding, sash windows, and an S brand engraved in the hand-carved porch posts. Dust devils, tumbleweeds swirl in the hot summer air. Rattlesnakes skulk about the empty plank corrals while an abandoned wooden hay rake deteriorates in the sun. A wooden water tower tilts, threatening to collapse into a pile of dark boards. Coyotes and wind are the only audible sounds. An unlettered tombstone lies nearby, the final place of two stagecoach robbers shot at the ranch, or so legend has it.

The Shirk brothers drove steers from Texas to populate the empty range. They controlled hundreds of square miles by owning the water holes and springs. They built an empire, fought Indians, range fires, and range wars. A blizzard killed three-quarters of their stock in a single winter.

In the end, the land rejected them. Only remnants remain of vast herds. The antelope and native grasses seek to return. The ranch has reverted to the ownership of the government. Near the rim rocks, the skeletons of cattle bleach in the sun and mix with the indifferent dust of the wind of the beginning.

TWENTY-SIX

The Sheep Bridge

*Mike my boy, come straight to Lake
County, don't bother stopping in America at
all.*
—An Irishman's note to his nephew

NEAR THE TOWN OF LAKEVIEW, a log sheep bridge used to cross my favorite fishing stream in the rugged canyon of Deep Creek, a long-time reminder of the great sheep herds that once grazed the high desert lands of eastern Oregon. Behind our place near town also stood a shearing shed: a long, narrow building of rustic planks and a shake roof. Each spring the Irish herded their flocks into plank corrals while Native Americans and Mexicans or gypsies camped nearby to work a few days shearing the sheep. Shearing occurred late enough in spring for lambing season to be finished. The male lambs that had survived late blizzards and coyotes faced one last test: cropping. After the bloody removal of testicles, large pans of Rocky Mountain "oysters" were taken to the herders' wagons for cooking—a rare delicacy.

The dirty, woolly sheep entered one end of the shearing shed and emerged at the other white and looking somewhat cold, with a brand painted on what little wool remained on their bodies. Large bails of wool accumulated near the shed for shipment to the mills at Pendleton. This was a nervous time for the herders and dogs because there was little for them to do. The character of the flocks also changed because of the corrals, and this change upset the dogs and herders, so attuned were they to the mood and condition of the flocks. The sheep, it seemed to me, became subject to a sort of group sheep psychosis consisting of fear, paranoia, disorientation, and a longing for the freedom of the range.

Our place and the shearing shed stood near the end of the railroad in Lake County, so we saw thousands of sheep and cattle crowded into the wood corrals for shipment south to markets in San Francisco. Even though the heyday of the sheep industry in Lake County was long past by the early 1940s, the rail head was the shipping terminal for a range larger than the state of Connecticut, and it is still astonishing to me the numbers of livestock that passed near our home. The sheep were packed into corrals so tight that the dogs could walk on their backs and never touch the ground. (I often saw them do this. Sometimes if the dogs found an opening, they would drop down into the pen, much to the consternation of the sheep.) During shipping season, the air was filled with thick Irish brogue, checks and cash changed hands, and whiskey flasks were passed around. After the excitement of shearing season, the shearing shed reverted to its usual role of hay storage and the scene of our endless cowboy-and-Indian cap-gun shootouts after the Saturday Roy Rogers and Gene Autrey matinees.

At Deep Creek, a bridge formerly used by sheep and stock. The structure no longer exists. *(Photo from the author's collection)*

Our neighbor, Dennis O'Callahan, kept of flock of a few hundred sheep year-round on his place. The shed sheltered the flock from the blizzards and incessant west winds of winter; I remember the mournful bleating of the sheep fading in and out of my consciousness at night with each gust of the bitter wind. Dennis was very hard to understand because of his thick Irish accent, but I did manage to learn that he had survived the great earthquake in San Francisco and that he had a wife and daughter there. For all the almost twenty years I knew him, I do not recall him leaving the Oregon desert or his family ever coming to visit him. I liked to work for him because he always paid with silver dollars retrieved from coffee cans buried outside his shack. After the shearing season, his abode would be frequented by the ladies from Roberta Avenue—what passed for a red light district in Lakeview. It was still later after the shearing season that he would deliver gifts of new, bright wool blankets made from his wool at the mill in Pendleton. Dennis earned a reputation for his prodigious capacity to drink whiskey, yet he lived to a ripe old age. My mother once found him buried in a snowbank in a blizzard outside his shack, but he revived, apparently too pickled to actually freeze.

The sheep industry in the Great Basin started after the excitement of the California Gold Rush: after about 1870 most of the Basque argonauts realized they would not get rich with gold and began herding sheep on the open ranges of Nevada, Oregon, Idaho, and Utah. The land was open and free to use at that time, providing an opportunity for landless, ambitious young men to build a large flock and perhaps a fortune. Lake County, Oregon, was an exception to the rest of the Great Basin: an enclave of Irish sheepmen in a largely Basque occupation. The Irish, sheep, and cattle began arriving in the county about 1869 after the Indian wars in the region were finished, and by 1875 cattle and sheep were numerous in the Summer Lake and Silver Lake valleys.

The cattle and sheep initially arrived from the Rouge River Valley, another example of back migration to the east. Exceptions were the Shirk brothers' cattle driven from Texas and the Pete French cattle herded by Mexican vaqueros and a Chinese cook from the Sacramento Valley. The Irish came directly from County Cork, Ireland, via the east coast or by way of San Francisco. The stock industry grew so fast that from 1878 to 1882, thousands of cattle were shipped to markets in San Francisco, often from the Nevada rail head of Winnemucca. By 1900 Lake County was home to 110,000 sheep and 26,000 cattle and horses. This rapid buildup of stock was not without setbacks. By 1905 the open range was so overgrazed that federal grazing regulation began on Forest Service lands.

In addition to overgrazing, numerous other problems—both natural and human—plagued the stock owner. As late as 1880, grizzly bears killed one hundred head of cattle near Paisley; in 1889 a serious range fire in the Warner Valley destroyed range for three thousand cattle; and the terrible winter of 1879-80 killed up to seventy-five percent of the cattle and forty percent of the horses on the ranges of eastern Oregon. Competition for range land also created conflict between sheepmen and cattlemen despite their often common Irish heritage. In north Lake County, over two thousand sheep were slaughtered on the range in 1902, and the mysterious murder of J.C. Conn may have been related to this range war. The Great Depression and the increased regulation imposed by the passage of the Taylor Grazing Act in 1934 only served to hasten the end of the great sheep industry on the Oregon high desert ranges, although a brief rebound occurred during World War II. Only the stockmen who were shrewd enough to buy scattered parcels with springs or water holes, effectively enabling them to control large areas of adjacent federal land, were able to survive the new economic order of the range.

The sheepherder never attained the mythic status the cowboy enjoyed in the American West, yet the job was equally dangerous and required as much or more skill. Cattle were released on the range and left unattended for extended periods, but sheep required constant attention day and night, month after month. The result was a unique, personal, and largely intuitive working partnership between sheepherder, sheep dog, and horse. It was unthinkable, for instance, to separate a herder from his dog except at the request of the herder.

To accommodate the need for the herder to live on the range for months on end, the sheepherder's arc was created—a wagon with iron-rimmed wooden wheels capable of being pulled by a horse or a pick-up truck. The wagon was a wooden box with a canvas cover containing a bed, a stove, a table, and a food cabinet to provide comfort for the herder and his dog. The arc was moved during the season as the flock was moved to fresh pasture; an aspen grove with a spring was often a favorite camping spot. While camped in aspen groves, herders often carved records of their presence in the soft white bark of the trees; many of the engravings remain visible today.

While in the outback, herders were alone with two thousand or more sheep, with the owner possibly bringing supplies once or twice a week. This often precluded the shepherd from having a normal family life while ensuring loneliness. Sometimes a herder would become "sagebrushed" and abandon the camp and the sheep. Some died of illness or untreated snake bites, or froze to death in blizzards. It was not unheard of for sheepherders to succumb to alcohol. When they did get to town, they often squandered their earnings on prostitutes or gambling. Lambing season was a particularly difficult time for the herders because a late spring storm could kill lambs in a matter of minutes. It is incredible that, despite the adversities, many herders loved their way of life. In this day, their profession is as threatened as that of the cowboy. Few traditional herders remain, and today, ironically, the relatively urban areas of the Willamette Valley host far more sheep than the endless ranges of the Oregon desert.

The shearing shed is now a long pile of dark, jumbled planks with protruding rusty nails. The rail head corrals are gone, as are the sheep and the men who worked them, along with much of the original West, though Dennis O'Callahan's shack still stands—unoccupied.

TWENTY-SEVEN

Ahab and the Cowboys

Thou canst not see my face: for there shall
no man see me, and live.
—Exodus 33:20

TWO TERRAINS have arguably defined the American character more than any other: the sea and the open prairies and deserts of the West. These, at least for a time, defined our cultural heroes, behavioral codes, and the concept of progress. For me, the terrain of the West has also defined my concept of God.

In *Moby Dick*, the classic American novel of the sea, its descriptive, almost scientific chapters about the sea, its animals, and the technology of whaling are in juxtaposition with the chapters of an epic human tale: a quest in a treacherous and unpredictable seascape. Perhaps Ahab was not really embarked on a quest for vengeance for a leg lost to the great white whale; perhaps he was on a spiritual quest, one that according to many religious traditions is always dangerous and usually fatal.

The white whale is the epitome of a defined, powerful, intelligent, self-willed entity from the churning chaos that is at the root of all creation and all nature. When Ahab got too close to the whale, the embodiment of the god of nature, he lost his life and the life of his crew save Ishmael: the sole survivor of the vicious struggle between man and god left to witness to the rest of humankind. Ahab sought to share in the god's powers only to be rejected by an indifferent and self-willed consciousness more powerful than his own. The whale roams the boundless matrix of creation from which it came to serve its own purposes and ends. Heaven help the man who tries to tie a line to the white god. When Ahab is at last defeated in his quest to capture the powers of the god, he is tangled in lines and harpoons on the back of the whale, looking for all the world like the crucified Christ on his cross. It is a scene well portrayed in the movie version of the book; in the end, all of the technology—gear, weapons, vessels—used to hunt the whale was of no avail, nor was Ahab's will. *Moby Dick* should be on the bookshelf of every scientist, environmentalist, and religious person because in it we get an unromantic idea of what God and nature are really like.

From the great spaces of the American West—the prairies, grasslands, deserts, and sage deserts—emerges the quintessential American hero: the cowboy. The cowboy contends with a landscape of range fires, flash floods, stampedes, blizzards, dust storms, and droughts as dangerous and unpredictable as Ahab's rolling sea. The voyagers on this western sea first encountered and then virtually eliminated the herds of buffalo, including a few rare albinos which to the Native Americans were deities not unlike Ahab's white whale. The buffalo were supplanted by herds of cattle themselves barely emergent from the wild canyons and ranges of the western grass and sage sea. Even the cowboy's mount had to be broken, tamed, trained, and maintained in control by a technology of skill, saddle, lariat, and bridle: tools similar in purpose to the gear and lines of Ahab's whaling vessel.

To encounter and subdue the raw, untamed beasts of nature, the cowboy developed a code involving courage and ritual not unlike the ritual on a whaling or military vessel. The code ranged from the general (do not shoot women or unarmed men) to the specific (never turn and wave when leaving someone on the range because they might feel you do not trust them). The code, the tack, the courage, the practice, the hierarchy were all necessary to cope with the ravaging forces all around in weather, terrain, and beast. So demanding was this life on the early range, a working cowboy did not expect many years of productive riding. Only in the exuberant release of a visit to town was the discipline relaxed, though even then the code was merely transferred to another western icon, the small-town sheriff.

In eastern Oregon, cowboys are called buckaroos, a name which designates more skill and toughness than that of an ordinary cowboy. As a youngster growing up in buckaroo country, I acted out the code in shootouts with imaginary bad guys using cap guns. This action occurred on Saturday afternoons on the way home from the weekly Roy Rogers, Gene Autrey, and Lone Ranger movies. My favorite grounds for this derring-do were the corrals and shearing sheds at the railhead. The code as interpreted by Hollywood at the time established clear boundaries between right and wrong, good guys and bad guys. Certain manners and behaviors were expected which today have dissolved into a cultural miasma as unpredictable and disconcerting as any high-desert blizzard. The code of the Lone Ranger, which today would seem naive to almost any youngster, was then taken seriously by us kids and even a few adults: to be fair, honest, caring, respectful, loyal, tolerant, morally courageous, and beholden to duty. Our scoutmasters took full advantage of the similarity between the cowboy code and the Boy Scout Oath to encourage many of us to become Eagle scouts.

In the sculpture of Frederic Remington, the cowboy can be seen fully defined, chiseled, and distinguished from the elemental nature that prevailed all around him. The cowboy in Remington's art looks like a Greek Apollo: the ideal form of maleness, power, control, and technique. This male icon is about as far from the pagan, female earth and stone from which it was chiseled as it is possible to get. The movie clichés of the cowboy eschewing the attractions of the female who would have him remain in town close to family and home, or riding off into the sunset after kissing the girl but little more, or restlessly pursuing the gods found in weather, beasts, and bad men, were perhaps images not too far from the truth.

There are at least two notable exceptions in the work of Remington to the triumphant form of the cowboy. In *End of the Trail*, a tired, defeated Indian warrior and his mount slump down almost kneeling to the ground, their identities slowly dissolving in fatigue back into the matrix of raw stone from which they emerged. In *The Norther*, a cowboy and his mount similarly dissolve, defeated not by the enemy, but by the vicious, cutting turmoil of nature itself.

I do not think the journey of the cowboy was primarily an economic quest any more than the final journey of Ahab was a quest for vengeance. The sale of whale oil or cattle became merely a means to an end to those who toiled on the sea and on the range. The cowboy's quest was at its core a spiritual quest. It was the search for the holy grail, the shaman's flight, the monk's chant, the burning bush.

Today a few family-owned ranches try to continue a way of life in the face of a government bureaucracy that owns most of the land in the West, the sometimes legitimate claims of environmentalists, corporate agriculture, and erratic prices. Their quest is only secondarily economic, a means to an end. Some of them hold onto at least a remnant of the code, but it weakens every day. The code and a way of life are held in tension between a pathological social order on the one hand and the wild gods of nature on the other. The wild beasts watch from the brush.

As Camille Paglia has stated, "There is danger in beauty." The poet Rainer Maria Rilke put it even more clearly: "Beauty is nothing but the beginning of terror." Ahab and the cowboys were fatally attracted to the primordial beauty of places they could not leave, ignore, or reject. At the same time they could not surrender fully to the seductive, sensuous pull of these terrains. Once they laid eyes on the sea and on the land of the West, their fates were sealed. Perhaps it is as the biblical author of Exodus wrote. In the end, they were consumed because one cannot see God and live.

TWENTY-EIGHT

Graves

We bind to you
at times frightened
that your abundance will
at night
roll over and crush us,
but then you stretch your
branches over us
like a home.

I FOUND THEIR NAMES neatly handwritten in the official journal of new Fort Warner, infants, women, soldiers, and the unknown: Charles Myer, Samuel Robbins, James Kingston, Laurence Trainer, Charles Williams, Robert Martin, William Watson, Michael Kennedy, John Sagstetter, Ellen Pollack, Nora Wilson, Catherine Wheaton, Unknown, Unknown, Unknown, Infant. They were sent west to fight the hostile Modocs and Paiutes in the desert intersection of California, Oregon, and Nevada. I imagined the army mules, horses, wagons as they trudged the grass and sage desert, over rim rock and endless frozen lava. Unpredictable weather would have plagued them—dust, heat, rain, freezing wind, and snow were all possible in the same day at the same place. I imagined the Mexican drivers whipping the teams to greater effort to carry baggage, food, a sawmill, officers' wives, and children all bound for new Fort Warner.

When they arrived they lived for a time on dirt floors; the winter snow and wind seeped into their shelters and their souls. The snow drifts cut their routes. There was no mail, no supplies, for days and weeks. Some soldiers got scurvy, some wives died in childbirth, and some children died soon after. The snow and wind became a more deadly enemy than the Indians.

But some found beauty in the clouds and sky, in the sunsets and aspen groves, in the high pines and spring flower meadows—the voices of the land seeped into the jagged cracks on their faces and hands. They found animals in unimaginable abundance: antelope, deer, mountain sheep; the calling clouds of ducks, geese, and cranes; little streams packed with trout. They found the coyote's yap, the cougar's cry, the grizzly's roar.

Some found pity for the hostiles being slaughtered like the animals. Some admired the braves who refused to surrender at the feet of General Crook. They began to look into the land's heart and saw in it their own wild and free impulse: a terrible, frightening abundance. Extremes permeated every day until there was no difference between the soul of the land and their own.

They ended in violence, in sickness, in exposure and in war, surrounded by a white picket fence in a land so lonely the survivors could not bear to leave them there. Their bones were later exhumed and reburied in San Francisco and Vancouver, Washington. One soldier, John Foley, a civil war veteran and Indian fighter from Cork County, Ireland, was court-martialled, busted from corporal to private, fined, and put inside the guardhouse. He was discharged from the army, but left no family or homestead, only an unmarked grave in Lakeview. On a recent Memorial Day, local veterans marked his grave with a headstone.

Today I feel their presence in the groves and quaking leaves. I do not carve the bark of the aspen with their initials lest they bleed once again.

TWENTY-NINE

Dr. Daly

It is my earnest desire to help, aid and assist
worthy and ambitious young men and women
of my beloved county of Lake, to
acquire a good education.
—Dr. Bernard Daly

H IS SCULPTURED HEAD stands on the pedestal where I saw it my first
day at Lakeview High School over forty years ago. A brass name-
plate identifies him as Dr. Bernard Daly. He stands just outside the high
school auditorium with its hardwood floors and rustic, bare interior; the
smell of first-day-of-school wax still permeates the building. His bust gives
the impression of a man looking far off into time and space. The picture
of him I found in the historical file at the museum reveals a young, handsome man exuding intelligence, but in the bust he seems older and wiser
than when I first saw him, perhaps a reflection of my own passages. His
life changed mine profoundly.

Dr. Daly was a universal man in ways not possible in this present specialized world, and he was exceptional even in his time. His titles extend
in a long list: doctor, lawyer, state legislator, rancher, architect, city plan-
ner, banker, candidate for Congress, judge, school board member, college
regent, businessman, and, after death, philanthropist. The high school he
designed, which I attended, is still in use today. The building he constructed
for the bank he founded survived the fire of 1900—the only business structure in town to do so. The railroad depot he sited still stands, albeit now
serving as a private residence. He was instrumental in building the Catholic
church in Lakeview, a structure in use today. Daly established the profitable

7T Ranch north of Warner Valley, an asset that contributed greatly to his wealth. He also became a prominent politician in eastern Oregon, due in large part to the influence his Irish and Southern origins had with the many Confederate Irish who emigrated to Lake County after the Civil War. Although Daly eventually ran for the United States Congress as a Democratic Party candidate, he failed to be elected.

Little is known about Dr. Daly's early years or his family. He was born in Ireland in 1858 and arrived in the United States when he was six years old. His parents settled near Selma, Alabama. Their son moved northward to attend normal school in Ohio and medical school at the University of Louisville. Daly served in the army and was discharged at Fort Bidwell in the northeastern corner of California. For unknown reasons, he traveled over the Warner Mountains and began practice in Lake County. The doctor became noted for his business acumen, his frugality, and his devotion to the land and people of the county. He never married and had no children, but he was not celibate; he left money in his will to his common law wife, a school teacher, who outlived him by thirty-eight years. When Dr. Daly died in January 1920 in a railroad passenger car near Stockton, California, while en route to San Francisco for medical treatment, his estate was valued at over seven hundred thousand dollars, a significant fortune at that time.

The most often-told story about the physician begins in the small ranching town of Silver Lake on Christmas Eve in 1894. About 160 people gathered in the community center on the second floor of the general store. During the event, a man overturned a kerosene lamp, causing the hall to quickly become engulfed in smoke and flames. The only exit was blocked, the stairs to the second floor collapsed under the weight of too many people, and those who jumped from a small window onto a porch also encountered disaster as the porch collapsed. Forty people were killed, three fatally burned, and many others injured. Immediately after the fire broke out, a young buckaroo named Ed O'Farrell began one of the most legendary rides in the history of the Pacific Northwest, covering the one hundred miles to Lakeview in nineteen hours in the dead of winter over almost nonexistent roads. As he rode to fetch Dr. Daly, ranches along the route provided fresh horses and were alerted to have buggies hitched for the doctor's return trip. O'Farrell reached Lakeview at four in the evening of Christmas Day; Dr. Daly left immediately, arriving in Silver Lake on the morning of December 26. He is credited with saving the lives of many injured by the fire, though O'Farrell shares the credit for heroism.

Today, the trip from Lakeview to Silver Lake requires less than two hours in the comfort of an automobile. It is difficult for me to imagine the sheer toughness and courage to ride the route at night, in winter, with no lights or roads for guidance. On a stone monument in the cemetery at Silver Lake, the names of the fire victims are engraved, but I can also imagine a statue of Ed O'Farrell leaning forward in the saddle at a gallop with snow and wind swirling about and a look of pure benevolent intent in his eyes. Perhaps someday such a monument will be built.

A less well-known story connected with Dr. Daly provides a glimpse into what was believed about his character. This tale begins with a bunch of cowboys rounding up stray cattle in the Lost Forest of northern Lake County. One of the men, while waiting for the others near Sand Springs, walked about with his horse to keep warm in the desert wind. A dull golden rock caught his attention, and some months later he left it with Dr. Daly, who at the time was also the judge. When Judge Daly had the rock assayed, he discovered it was fifty percent gold. Despite spreading word around the county in an effort to report this outcome to the cowboy, the man was never found. Dr. Daly went so far as to leave a provision in his will that the cowboy be paid for the gold should he ever return. This story portrays the mythic proportions of the doctor's character in the minds of the residents of the region.

Of all the remarkable accomplishments of Dr. Daly, none surpasses his bequest of a scholarship fund to enable the youth of Lake County to attend the public college or university of their choice in the state of Oregon. As a result of his generosity, thousands of the sons and daughters of mill workers, cattlemen, loggers, and other blue-collar laborers have become lawyers, doctors, teachers, scientists, pilots, and professionals in all walks of life. Because of Dr. Daly, I was able to attend college, study science, and avoid an otherwise sure destiny in the sawmills where my father spent his life.

The children walking by look at me curiously as I touch the sculpted head of Dr. Daly and say thank you. I know the town they live in is slowly dying. In the bright international economy of Oregon, the rural towns face unemployment rates five times that of Eugene or Portland. This town seems unable to adapt to the decline of the economies of extraction, cutting, mining, and grazing. Over half the homes are substandard, and most of the children will have to get an education and move to the cities to find a future. I wonder, which of them will Dr. Daly rescue?

PART SIX

HISTORY

THIRTY

Boat on a Dry Lake

Moonlight inscribes
the lake in gold, a goose call
ascends,
my heart beats
on the shore of night.

I WAS ABOUT EIGHT YEARS OLD when my grade-school class visited the local museum in Lakeview and became acquainted with the boat
Lakeview. I remember pictures of it and a life buoy clearly marked
"Lakeview" hanging on the wall. Almost fifty years later on a visit to the
same museum, my interest was rekindled with questions.

How did such an elegant little boat, which looked like an offspring
of the ferries on San Francisco bay or Puget Sound, end up on a shallow
lake in the high desert of eastern Oregon? Why was it built, and why was
it placed on Goose Lake, which manages to completely dry up once or
twice each century? Like most stories from history in Lake County, I knew
the origin of the boat lay in some seemingly unrelated event, and that the
story would speak volumes about the general historical patterns of the
West and the character of the people involved in it. I was not disappointed.

The boat really began with a wagon road, a land rush, and a land fraud,
and it ended in the "bust" half of a "boom and bust" cycle so typical of
the history of the West. In 1864, Congress decided that a military wagon
road was needed between Boise, Idaho, and Eugene, Oregon. To enable
the road to be built, the government granted land to the Oregon Central
Military Road Company, including alternate sections for three miles on
each side of the road centerline. (Later the grant would be extended to

alternate sections six miles on each side.) The road inefficiently wandered throughout the high desert country of Oregon to include key watered areas in the private sections. It was so poor that General Crook, at the time of his Indian campaigns in the area, resorted to having his troops build the road, including the stone bridge across the narrows of the Warner Lakes. The road also dismembered the Klamath Indian Reservation, the land company gaining rights to Indian land in a decision by the "great" Justice Oliver Wendell Holmes. Today the route of the original road is clearly evident on government maps that reveal the orderly checkerboard of private and government ownership. The maps, aside from being orderly, reveal that no consideration was given to the ecological realities or topographic contours of the high desert. As a result, private holders often controlled much larger parcels of surrounding government lands by controlling access and water sources.

Following a complex history of sales and lawsuits, the Oregon Valley Land Company (as it was now called) had by 1908 secured 400,000 acres in Lake County. The company, seeking to profit by the consolidation of its holdings, announced that it would offer 11,992 parcels of from 10 to 1,000 acres with a building lot in the Lakeview town site thrown into the bargain with each parcel. The sale and resultant division of the land was completely oblivious to the climatic realities of the region in that few parcels of only 1,000 acres in most of Lake County could sustain a viable ranch or farm. The company announced a land auction in Lakeview to occur in 1909. Needless to say, local boosterism was at a high pitch, the future looked bright, and health and wealth were just around the corner. One minor problem presented itself: how to get the bidders into the desolate outback of Lake County?

In 1909, the great, shallow inland lake called Goose Lake presented a real problem to the Oregon Valley Land Company and its plan to bring land buyers to the auction. The lake occupied 194 square miles, averaged only eight feet in depth, and during dry years became a swamp. By 1909 the narrow-gauge Nevada, California and Oregon Railroad had only reached Alturas, California. There were no roads or railroads covering the fifty-five miles from Alturas to Lakeview, including the twenty-eight miles covered by the shallow waters of Goose Lake. To correct this problem, the land company began building a "road" between Alturas and the southern shore of Goose Lake, using horses and scrapers. Dickie and Dickie, a naval architectural firm from Oakland, California, was hired to design a ferry boat to operate on Goose Lake because the firm had experience in the design of larger boats for use on San Francisco Bay. The elegant little

Lakeview was designed after the model of its larger relatives that carried automobiles across the bay. The specifications called for the finest in marine materials—oak, pine, and brass—and were so detailed that they spelled out who was responsible for serving coffee and sandwiches on the trial trip.

Pieces of the *Lakeview* were hauled by wagon to the shore of Goose Lake and assembled by William Brusstar of San Francisco in just two months, only eleven days before the land auction in Lakeview required the boat's services. It was only sixty-four feet in length, but it included an upper open-air deck with enclosed pilot house and a lower deck capable of carrying a few automobiles. It was powered by twin thirty-horsepower marine gasoline engines and had a draft of only about four feet. Even with the shallow draft, operations on Goose Lake were hampered by the weed-filled waters, though the lake was full of water in 1909. To solve the problem of weeds tangling in the propeller screws, an Indian woman was hired to use her ancient skills and weave baskets to protect the screws. This solution apparently worked, but to operate the boat on the shallow lake, the land company was forced to build a three-hundred-feet-long pier at the south end of the lake and another eight hundred feet

The ferry *Lakeview* on the waters of Goose Lake, about 1909. *(Photo courtesy of the Oregon Historical Society.)*

long at the north end. The land company spent twenty thousand dollars on the boat and an unknown amount on the roads and piers.

The *Lakeview* succeeded in carrying one thousand land buyers to Lakeview, but the aftermath of the auction is familiar to students of the history of the West. Many people, including those in the east whose interests were represented by the land buyers at the auction, ended up owning a piece of paradise consisting of basalt rim rock, sage desert, and grassland. More often than not, the owners never saw the land they bought. To this day, the Lake County sheriff auctions tax-delinquent Oregon Valley Land Company parcels, but almost all of the auctioned land was eventually reacquired by local owners for reconsolidation into larger, economically viable plots. Most of the Oregon Valley Land parcels in Lakeview were never developed and today can be had for a few hundred dollars a lot. The home that my father built near Lakeview was built on such a lot, and he constantly worried about having clear title due to the complex legal history of land exchanges associated with the Lake County land rush. About the only beneficial remnant of the Oregon Valley Land Company is the Drews Valley Irrigation District and the dam and reservoir built by the company.

The pleasing little ferry *Lakeview* continued regular operations for about three years and operated intermittently until about 1924, but after the railroad reached Lakeview in 1912, its fate was sealed. It is not known what happened to the boat or where its remains lie. Perhaps they rest comfortably beneath the silt and weeds of the lake it so briefly plied, or perhaps the fine marine pine and oak were burned to warm the rooms of the early inhabitants of the Goose Lake Valley. The only intact remains are the original blueprints and specifications filed in the National Maritime Museum of San Francisco and copies of the same filed in my closet. There are also photos and the life buoy in the museum in Lakeview.

The eastern shore of Goose Lake remains my favorite place on earth. I like to imagine that after I am scattered in its waters, the *Lakeview* will be resurrected, its propellers churning above me in the mysterious play of light, wind, water, and time that is Goose Lake. Perhaps the band on the upper deck will play for the maiden voyage just as it did once before: the ladies in bonnets, the men in suits, and the future as colorful and promising as the golden West.

THIRTY-ONE

Lakeview After the Fire

Upon whose bodies the fire had no power,
nor was an hair of their head singed.
—Daniel 3:27

W HEN I FOUND the old black-and-white photograph in the museum, I wanted to have been there when it was taken. For some reason, such photographs exude mystery; the lack of color leaves so many questions unanswered, the imagination free to range over the possibilities of the past.

The picture was taken by someone the day after the great fire of 1900: the fire that destroyed the entire downtown of Lakeview in a single blaze that left a glow in the sky visible one hundred miles away. Only the brick skeleton of one business remained, a building still in use today. The picture reminds me of one that could have been taken after a war: a town center leveled as if bombed.

The photographer had climbed a ways up the foothills of the Warner Mountains to the east of town, the same slopes I sledded in the winter to the dismay of my parents, who could visualize only broken bones. What is unusual about the photo is the foreground where two men, barely visible, pose in front of the ruined town below as if a festive occasion were in progress—like the circus coming to town or the killing of a record buck deer or mountain lion.

What can explain the pose, the carefree indifference? The town was gone, no supplies or services closer than one hundred miles over poor roads. (The railroad had not yet reached Lakeview.) Only a few private residences remained on the outskirts. Perhaps the indifference lies with

The town of Lakeview after the devastating fire of 1900. *(Photo courtesy of the Lake County Historical Society.)*

the age of the men. They appear young, with the golden West spread out before them as an endless cornucopia of possibility, or resource, of potential wealth, of dreams. The pine forests in the Warner Mountains must have seemed trackless, the grazing meadows endless, the water pure and eternal, the soil deep and unbroken, the game and birds boundless, the fish in the lakes uncountable. In the new century of 1900, the world was not acquainted with two world wars, the Great Depression, or the dust bowl. The Civil War was behind the nation, and the industrial revolution was in full swing. Perhaps the reduction of the town to ashes seemed to them nothing more than a temporary inconvenience; what burned one day could be rebuilt tomorrow.

I believe the men in the photograph appear casual because they were infected with the great idea of the West. Any cataclysm could not dampen the experience of paradise, and, as such, the event became a photo opportunity. It is a picture born of the hubris of not having perceived any limits. If something was lost—a town, or a species, or a forest, or a wetland, or a meadow—there was another to take its place. The fire would presage a series of fires in the town that would burn down one sawmill after another. As a child, I witnessed two go up in flames; both were gone in less than an hour and rebuilt a few weeks later.

I wonder what the men in the photograph would think if they were alive today. In less than one hundred years, the forests of Lake County are so depleted that only one sawmill remains. The vast sheep herds are a memory. The list of endangered species grows longer. The only building downtown to survive the fire is used to sell insurance. Old photographs in black and white fade and crumble in the drawers of museums and libraries.

THIRTY-TWO

The Depot

The sawmill burner throws
skyward sparks,
temporary stars,
the moon too bright
for real stars.

I REMEMBER VISITING the old brick railroad depot as a child; the railway agent and his family were friends with my family. They lived in the upstairs of the depot that I knew even then was a unique building in the town. Both the agent, a man named Harry Watson, and my father were self-taught musicians, and many a Sunday afternoon was spent listening to the romantic ballads of Gene Autrey, Hank Williams, and Woody Guthrie. I also recall frequent visits alone to the railroad yards to hitch rides on the steam trains working the yard. More than once, when my mother discovered my whereabouts, I was spanked every third step all the way home with a willow switch, a procedure more damaging to my ego than to my hind end. More than once, the train engineer took mercy on me and talked my mother out of spanking me. Such was my fascination with trains that it was impossible for my parents to keep me away from them.

The depot was, like so many things in the Oregon desert, the termination of a failed dream. The story began about 1880 when the need for a railroad into Lake County was becoming apparent. The Modoc War was over and the ranches of Lake County were producing abundant herds of cattle, sheep, and even turkeys which had to be driven to the nearest rail heads in Reno or Winnemucca, Nevada, for shipment to the San Francisco Bay Area. (It is difficult for me to imagine trying to herd turkeys across the Oregon desert with the constant attention they must have drawn from coyotes, hawks, and cougars.) In response to the need, the Nevada and Oregon Railroad was born and Col. Thomas Moore hired to construct the road.

A dispute soon broke out over whether to extend the road north to Oregon, where the need was evident, or south from Reno. The dispute ended in the death of a Mr. Scoville, the company secretary, when a stock-holders' meeting turned into bedlam and a gunfight broke out. The event was the harbinger of difficult years for the railroad; a litany of lawsuits, labor disputes with Chinese workers, lost fortunes, personal tragedies, re-organizations, floods, blizzards, and financial disasters followed. By 1912 the railroad managed to reach Lakeview, where the dream of a route through eastern Oregon clear to the Dalles on the Columbia River would die forever.

By the time the newly named Nevada-California-Oregon railroad, known as the NCO or "Narrow, Crooked and Ornery," reached Lakeview, it was one of the longest narrow-gauge railroads in the twentieth century. Because of its ongoing difficulties, both physical and fiscal, it became known as the "Northern California Outrage" by its detractors. It was said that it was possible to get off the train anywhere between Reno and Lakeview, walk to the nearest ranch, have a meal, and get back on board without hurrying.

Despite its problems, the NCO would enable a brief "gold rush" to occur in the High Grade Mining District to the east of Goose Lake. The mining district, located on the Oregon-California border, climaxed in 1912 after giving rise to the boom town of High Grade in the Warner Mountains and to such legendary characters as High Grade Annie, a spirited woman who drove the ore wagon teams down the steep, crooked roads to the rail head near Goose Lake. Because of the NCO, the gold mines could bring supplies into the remote region and ship ore out.

The NCO for a time also contributed to a brief land rush and tour-ist mecca on the eastern shore of Goose Lake near New Pine Creek. A resort had been built on the lake shore, which at the time of its heyday in 1913 was said to rival Lake Tahoe in its beauty and physical setting, but today only pictures remain of the once famous Fairport Inn. Land promoters also sought to turn the east shore of Goose Lake at the border into a city: "Fairport—The city which is to be." The promotional materials portrayed Fairport as an agricultural paradise with vast orchards, no malaria, no fevers, no plague. The slogans were: "A Fairport Investment Sure and Safe," "Fairport is a Money Maker," and "Fairport is the loveliest spot in

California." Today the little village of New Pine Creek on the Oregon side of the border remains economically distressed and largely forgotten, though it is still beautiful.

By 1926, the NCO railroad had been taken over by the Southern Pacific and the track redone to standard gauge all the way to the terminus in Lakeview. The Southern Pacific would enable the vast timber resources of the Warner Mountains to the east and the forests across Goose Lake to the west to be brought into production. Numerous sawmills and wooden box factories came into existence, including the mill at Willow Ranch, California, and several mills and box factories in Lakeview. My father arrived at the Willow Ranch mill in the late 1930s, grateful to have a job during the throes of the Great Depression. Today all that remains of the mill is a picture my father took of it and a classic wood burner teepee still visible from Highway 395. During World War II and for a time thereafter, I remember seemingly endless stacks of lumber and warehouses full of wooden box materials in the railroad yard at Lakeview awaiting shipment to San Francisco and the vegetable and fruit regions of California. My father loaded wooden box "shook" onto box cars, and one summer I worked alongside him in the box factory. My memories of it include the unrelenting noise of the machinery and thick dust and darkness in the mill. Today only one sawmill remains active in all of Lake County; nothing remains of the box factory and sawmill where my father worked, nothing of the lumber yards and warehouses, nothing of the stock corral at the rail head. All that remains is the depot.

Lakeview has a number of old buildings with an interesting architectural history, but the depot is unique. The bank building downtown clearly reflects Greek influence with its columns and Parthenon-like front. The Alger theater remains in operation with its clear art deco influences. The Methodist Church and the Utley mansion might have been lifted into place directly from Tuscany, so strong is the influence of the Italian stone cutters who constructed them. The Forest Service buildings at Paisley and the Hart Mountain Wildlife Refuge reflect the sturdy stone and wood construction of the depression-era Civilian Conservation Corps. But the NCO depot brought to the wind-strafed desert of eastern Oregon a touch of the romance of the California mission.

In the 1880s, a style known as Mission Revival surfaced in the architecture of California, including buildings at Stanford University and the Mission Inn at Riverside. The style consisted of solid massive walls with buttressing, broad unadorned wall surfaces, terraced bell-towers, and pierced companarios (mission belfry facades), according to Kevin Palmer, an author who has studied the style. Travelling inland from coastal California and then northward to the NCO buildings in Alturas, California, the Mission Revival style finally reached the little depot in Lakeview. The agent for this journey was San Francisco architect Carl Werner, a graduate of MIT who specialized in the design of Masonic temples. Hired by the NCO to design its administration building in Alturas, which was constructed from 1917 to 1918, Werner may also have designed the Lakeview depot, although this has not yet been proved. The NCO administration building, complete with low-pitched tile roof, parapet in the center, and arches in the entryway, clearly reflects his avant-garde Mission Revival style. The Spanish colonial features of the building include ornate molding over the doors, a center window on the facade, and a bell tower which housed a wooden bell. The little depot at Lakeview mirrors the style on a much smaller scale, including a low-pitched tile roof with buttresses, wide overhanging eaves, ornate arch windows over the doors, a porch with Roman-like aqueduct arches, and a companario-like facade at the south end of the building. The depot also has thick walls, albeit of brick. Eventually the Mission Revival style transformed into a more Mediterranean Spanish-Italian emphasis, but a little of the revival remains, forgotten out on the Oregon desert.

Today the Lakeview depot exists as a private residence, the administration building still stands in Alturas, but the Southern Pacific closed the Alturas-to-Lakeview route of the original NCO. The railroad was bought by Lake County with the use of state lottery funds and renamed the Goose Lake 55. (The route is fifty-five miles from Alturas to Lakeview. The name was chosen as the winning entry of a naming contest, submitted by a young woman from Lakeview High School.) The railroad still operates today on a very limited basis; the financial difficulties of the original NCO continue. No passenger trains travel the fifty-five miles along the shores of Goose Lake as they once did in the heyday of Lake County, but the route remains in surroundings wild, beautiful, and undiluted in the high mountain light, open to the romantic dreams of the pioneers who imagined it, to dreams of the steam train, the bounding deer, and the endless flocks of birds on the gleaming waters of Goose Lake.

THIRTY-THREE

Wigwams and Pond Monkeys

Yet man is born unto trouble, as the sparks fly upward.
—Job 5:7

M Y FATHER CONSIDERED HIMSELF LUCKY to have surveyed dam sites and painted bridges on the Oregon coast during the Great Depression, but in the late 1930s he ventured with a dependent mother and sister to the shores of Goose Lake to work in a sawmill and wooden box factory. He spent most of the rest of his life in such mills.

Contrary to the myth of popular culture, the West was not primarily the domain of the free-riding cowboy; most of the men and women worked in mines, sawmills, canneries, railroad yards, slaughterhouses, and factories. The work was dirty, back-breaking, and dangerous. To this day, the job of timber faller is one of the most dangerous, and more than one of my classmates died young under a log or fallen tree. Medical and life insurance were unheard of, though the mills where my father worked would pay to stitch up a man who lost a finger or hand on the job. Few of the older men in the mills possessed all of their fingers.

My father's work ranged from tending boilers and stacking shook in the warehouse to acting as a "pond monkey" and night watchman. The night watchman job was solitary and necessary since mills often caught fire, and when they did, they went up like a torch. My father was best suited to being a pond monkey because the job required someone small and agile to walk on the floating logs, push them towards the mill with long pike poles, and see to it that they caught on the conveyor chain that pulled them into the mill. In my father's day, the ponderosa pine logs were large and did not easily roll—but if they did, a pond monkey, if not well-balanced, could drown or be crushed. I also remember my father's stint as a boiler tender. In his day the mill wasted about half of the raw log; the waste sawdust, bark, and blocks or trimmings were used to feed the steam boilers that operated the mill machinery. When the steam was up, there was often more than enough fuel, so the waste was sent by conveyor to large metal tepee-shaped burners called wigwams. The wigwams belched smoke and hot cinders when the mill was in operation.

My father and the people he worked with in the mill considered themselves "stiffs" or "working stiffs"; they talked a lot about the "school of hard knocks," and most of them sought for their children the education that they lacked. They spoke to the young people about the perils of a life in the mill, and some of the youngsters listened. (There were only two skilled jobs in the mill: the millwright and the saw filer.) They were often unionized, but the mill either worked them long hours of overtime or laid them off with the constant "boom and bust" cycles so prevalent in the West. They had no pension, and when they retired, they were totally dependent on social security. For most of them, Franklin Roosevelt enjoyed the status of a savior.

I worked with my father one summer in the mill. The place was incredibly dark, dusty, noisy, and hot. I was warned to duck behind stacks of shook when the saw blades broke and sent metal flying around the mill like shrapnel. I still think of the mill as the realization of hell on earth. I far preferred surveying roads or even fighting forest fires than the confinement of a mill job.

In many parts of the West, the metal wigwams are the last standing reminder of the legendary era of the sawmills. I remember when learning to fly light planes that the wind direction and speed could invariably be determined by the black or white smoke from the wigwams of the small mill towns below. Although many small towns which lost their mills like to blame "tree huggers," the fact is that the mills were doomed by a combination of technological change, over-cutting of the forests, and the coming of a global economy. The remaining mills today are more likely to employ a computer programmer than a laborer to manage the computer-controlled equipment necessary to cut much smaller logs. I still think of the wigwams as a Western symbol of waste, extraction, and decline. Today a wigwam still stands at the mill site at Willow Ranch, California, on the shore of Goose Lake where my father first became a mill worker, but that is all that stands.

THIRTY-FOUR

The Balloon War

I look back to them
softening to trees;
look back to their
sadness
too soft for a hard land.

I T IS A TESTAMENT to the hubris and desperation of war that children were used to make weapons of death to kill other children. Sometime between November 3, 1944, and early April 1945, a hydrogen-filled balloon made of paper by school children was launched from one of twenty-one stations on the eastern seacoast of the Japanese island of Honshu. It was one of ninety-three hundred bombing balloons sent eastward as part of the war effort by the Japanese to attack the Americans. The Japanese were desperate for a means to retaliate for the Doolittle raid on Japan and for the disaster at the battle of Midway.

A plan was conceived to use the jet stream, a river of air at high altitude not well-understood at the time, to carry the war to the western United States. Ultimately, at least 285 balloons or parts of balloons would be found as far east as Michigan and as far south as Mexico. Most landed as intended on the Pacific Northwest in forested areas. One of these would settle into the pines and firs above the high desert of eastern Oregon near what is now the Gearhart Wilderness Area. This one balloon wrote a little-known but tragic chapter in the story of a brutal war raging around the world.

The idea of a balloon bomb originated in Japan in 1933, but its practicality for use against the United States had to wait for meteorologists to understand the wind currents that blow from west to east across the

Pacific Ocean at speeds of from one hundred to two hundred miles per hour in the winter months. Later, long after the war, the jet stream would become useful in making accurate weather forecasts. In 1943, it was not well-charted, leading the Japanese to launch some two hundred paper test balloons that winter.

The Japanese had to solve several technical problems to make the balloons stable in the jet stream. They were to fly at over thirty-thousand feet for several days in order to reach the western United States, but during the day hydrogen gas would expand in the balloon, causing it to rise or even burst, while at night the gas cooled and contracted, causing it to sink or even fall into the sea. The problem was solved by using a gas discharge valve during the day and by dropping ballast during the night. To solve weight problems, the balloons were made from tissue paper using fibers of the kozo bush, a member of the mulberry-tree family. Four plies made the top of the balloon and three the bottom; the plies were joined by an adhesive made from potato paste. The Japanese children used as labor to construct the paper shells were often so hungry that they were caught eating the paste intended for balloon construction.

A balloon of thirty-two feet in diameter was designed to provide the buoyancy needed to lift both anti-personnel and incendiary bombs. The Japanese hoped to set the forests of the Pacific Northwest ablaze to tie up manpower and throw the population into a panic. The United States government realized this threat and secretly devised "Project Firefly," which placed about three thousand black paratroopers and a number of transport aircraft on alert to combat fires. "Project Lightning" was devised to alert agricultural offices, colleges, 4-H clubs, and veterinarians to be on the lookout for signs of livestock or crop disease, since there was also a concern that the balloons could carry biological or chemical weapons.

Ultimately only two balloons would be shot down over the continent, but the best defense against them turned out to be secrecy. The military, the press, and the public remained silent when balloons were found. The Japanese received so little information about their attacks that they considered the program to be ineffective and discontinued it. Although a military failure, one balloon landed on the power lines connecting the secret nuclear reactors at Hanford, Washington, with the Grand Coulee Dam, shutting down the reactors for three days due to a power failure. The result was a delay in the race to make plutonium for the nuclear weapon that would ultimately destroy Nagasaki.

On May 5, 1945, the Reverend and Mrs. Archie Mitchell and five children from the small logging community of Bly, Oregon, drove for a picnic in the secluded forests near Gearhart Mountain. The Reverend Mitchell, while parking the car, heard an explosion. He quickly discovered the torn bodies of his wife and the five children. They had found a Japanese balloon and had triggered one of the bombs, although the incendiary bombs did not explode. The deaths of these six Americans were the only casualties due to enemy action to occur on United States soil during World War II.

Today a rock monument with a brass plaque stands near a forest road in the Gearhart Mountains; I drove past it many times in connection with my summer duties as a Forest Service road surveyor. In the summer of 1976, seventy-one-year-old Sakyo Adachi, Japanese designer of radio equipment for the balloons, visited the site to pay respects and to seek a measure of redemption. On Saturday, May 6, 1995, a ceremony was held at the monument to remember the incident fifty years before in the remote Oregon forest. While not a major event in the vast configuration of destruction and death that was World War II, it was and is a symbol that requires from us further redemptive acts, including remembrance, a symbol of a war where children made weapons and children died because of the acts of their parents. I often visit the forest I know and love to honor it and those forever a part of it. Perhaps partial compensation for a short life is to reside in a place of beauty.

THIRTY-FIVE

Naming the Desert

I love things lost, lonely,
stark and spare;
it is possible I will love you.

I HAVE FINISHED my days and nights in the Oregon desert. There is a sense of loss as I close my book of chapters. I see now that as a child I caught a glimpse of fragments, of death throes, of the end of the West and of innocence, perhaps even the end of a kind of paradise. Still, I do not want to romanticize my childhood: the storms when we were isolated for days and the only way out was on snowshoes; the cold outdoor toilets; the constant tending of wood stoves for heat, cooking, and wash water; the seasonal slaughter of animals, both domestic and wild, to survive; the ill-nesses when we could not afford a doctor. Is it possible to love the inju-ries of the past? Is it possible to love a place and a time and the deformities in them perhaps even too much?

I learned the history and geography of the Oregon desert after I left it, but it still fascinates me because amidst all the wreckage both human and natural, an essential transcendence remains: of a kid growing up poor near the corrals and sheep sheds on the other side of the tracks, of escape from a father whose dreams lay unfulfilled in the daily grind of sawmill work, of the transcendent flight of the shamans engraved on the desert while all around lies the transcendence of the evening's purple glow on the overgrazed grasslands, a light that not all the cutting, digging, graz-ing, and draining has been able to cloud or erase. The desert now seems even more like a mother. The desert rim rocks seem more like her bones, as the ancients thought, and the stars of the Milky Way seen from the desert seem more alive with the spirits of its departed inhabitants. The ability to again talk to the animals and to lie down upon the skin of the desert earth seems more urgent. More people of goodwill are falling in love with the desert, and the future prospects of restoration and redemption seem brighter. The animal wars are over, the soldiers are gone to their graves, and artists are locating the spiritual longitudes and latitudes of the desert.

It seems to me that the geography of the desert is misnamed. Most of the springs, dry lakes, wells, buttes, and creeks are named for people I did not know and will never know. I do not know if as people they were worthy of a spot on the geography of transcendence or whether they loved what was named for them, that which they almost destroyed. Perhaps the very naming is what destroyed, given the power of words, given that the breath of the namer is what creates. If the namers of the desert had at least loved what they named for themselves and destroyed, is there a small measure of redemption? Is there a small measure of redemption now that I know I loved what I helped destroy? Is there redemption for me from the porcupines I stoned and the deer I killed without need? Is there redemption for the magpie nests we tore up, the forests we felled, and the mines we tore into the earth and abandoned to the wind? Is there redemption from the excess of trout we killed without ceremonies of propitiation to the spirit of the redband trout? Is it right to eat the liver of the fresh-killed deer without prayer and ceremony to the earth from which it came? Is it right to drain the home of millions of teal and mallards without thought other than profit, to leave the drained marshes to dry in the sun? What are the necessary redemptive acts? Is it necessary to return and atone or is it sufficient to leave, to remember and to love the new place where one lives?

I do not think the shamans of the desert are finished with us; I know they are not finished with me. They will not allow a simple turning and walking away. Their intent is too strong; they lived too long mixed with the unbridled, wild, tumultuous forces of nature all around them to be ignored. Even our technology and our powerful elucidation of science cannot withstand the ultimate subtle hold and intent of the desert. The shamans extracted too much power from the gods of the desert to allow it to be wasted, ignored, and abandoned; the longer we stay, the more the shamans will prevail upon us, and as they do, we will harvest the desert for its silence, and profit from the music of its winds, and capitalize on its smell after a thundering rain, and market its eternal clarity of purpose, and take stock in its meanings, and luxuriate in its mineral waters.

I have come to think that the geography of the desert should be re-named with powerful, great, religious words—words like silence, incar-nation, detachment, exorcism, prayer, sacred, grace, god, fear, faith, ecstasy, worship, mystic, judgment, imagination, revelation, and heaven—words defined by Kathleen Norris in her book *Amazing Grace*. Long Lake would be named Sacred Lake because it was the launching ground for the sha-mans' trance-like flights of the soul; Deep Creek would be named Wor-ship Creek when the redband trout are restored and the waters are clean and roaring in the canyon because the god of trout is far more ancient than our own. The Warner Mountains would be named Revelation Moun-tains for the ever-changing revelations of light and storms; Hart Moun-tain would be named Mystic Mountain because of the storms that clothe it in mysterious snows in winter and brilliant blankets of flowers and sage in spring. Any number of springs could be named Sacred, so sacred is water in the desert. For those places where Native Americans were slaughtered without thought or mercy, Exorcism would be a suitable name to exor-cise this history. For the meadows, groves, and wild wet lands that remain in the desert, the names could be changed regularly from Grace to Faith to Prayer to Ecstasy because each day they are their own gods deserving of religious words. But there is one word that I will assign to the most frag-ile and beautiful remnant I can find in the desert. I search for it still—a place called Redemption.

Leaving Home

Can I find a home in
this endless time: where
is the beginning, the end?
Does some memory of things
loved on the sweet earth
survive?

T HE HOUSE MY FATHER BUILT still stands, but it is a shack. The grand flower garden my mother tended in the brief summers is covered with weeds. The barn we built is gone. There are no animals in the fenced fields.

The fir tree my father planted in the front yard the day I was born has flourished straight and tall. The shearing shed in the back has fallen into sheaves of old brown planks, and there are no sheep or corrals. The sawmill across the railroad tracks is gone. The mill pond is filled with gravel and dirt. There are no lumber piles scenting the air with cut pine. The camas meadow that was once nearby and beautiful in the spring is a barren lot. The house sags on its tentative foundation. I do not know if it will outlast me, but the ghosts and memories in it are exorcised. I feel relieved with no need to return.

But there are properties I have removed and taken with me, things from the desert and the house. I want to be like the desert: subtle, silent, and searched for. I want hidden meanings, to be rare as semaphore grass, unyielding as tui chub.

I do not want to be named or on a map. I do not want to be found by roads.

I want to lap in the waters of Goose Lake and glisten in the frigid night of stars: icy, clear, certain, eternal.

Selected Bibliography

Aikens, Melvin. *Archaeology of Oregon*. Portland: U.S. Department of Interior, 1993.

Aikens, Melvin, and Dennis Jenkins. *Fort Rock Archaeology Since Cressman*. Eugene: University of Oregon Department of Anthropology, 1994.

Allen, Barbara. "The Heroic Ride in the Pacific Northwest." *Columbia* (winter 1990): 16.

_____. *Homesteading the High Desert*. Salt Lake City: University of Utah Press, 1987.

Allison, Ira. *Geology of Pluvial Lake Chewaucan Lake County, Oregon*. Corvallis: Oregon State University Press, 1982.

_____. *Pluvial Fort Rock Lake, Lake County Oregon*. Portland: Department of Geology and Mineral Resources, 1979.

Alt, David, and Donald Hyndman. *Northwest Exposures: A Geologic Story of the Northwest*. Missoula: Mountain Press Publishing Co., 1995.

_____. *Roadside Geology of Oregon*. Missoula: Mountain Press Publishing Co., 1978.

Angulo, Jamie de. "The Achumawi Life-Force." *The Journal of California Anthropology* (1975): 60.

_____. "Achumawi Sketches." *The Journal of California Anthropology* (1974): 80.

Aveni, Anthony, ed. *Native American Astronomy*. Austin: University of Texas Press, 1977.

Bandi, Hans-Georg, et al. *The Art of the Stone Age*. New York: Crown Publishers, 1961.

Barrett, S.A. "The Material Culture of the Klamath Lake and Modoc Indians of Northeastern California and Southern Oregon." *University of California Publications in American Archaeology and Ethnology* (1910): 239-292.

Barry, Bob. *From Shamrocks to Sagebrush*. Lakeview: Examiner Publishing, 1969.

Barry, Patricia. "Ferry Boat in the Desert." *The Journal of the Modoc County Historical Society* (1980): 62.

_____. "Fairport—A Promotional Dream That Failed." *The Journal of the Modoc County Historical Society* (1987): 135.

_____. *In Search of Captain Warner*. Bend: Maverick Publications, 1995.

_____, ed. *The Journal of the Modoc County Historical Society: Nevada-California-Oregon Railway Issue* (1982).

Barter, Eloise. "Achumawi and Atsugewi Fishing Gear." *Journal of California and Great Basin Anthropology* (1990): 37.

Bastien, Joseph. *Mountain of the Condor: Metaphor and Ritual in an Andean Ayllu*. Prospect Heights: Waveland Press Inc., 1978.

Bean, Lowell John, ed. *California Indian Shamanism*. Menlo Park: Ballena Press, 1992.

Bedwell, Stephen. *Fort Rock Basin: Prehistory and Environment*. Eugene: University of Oregon Books, 1973.

Benson, Arlene, and Floyd Buckskin. "Magnetic Anomalies at Petroglyph Lake." *Rock Art Papers* 8 (1991): 53.

Blanquet, Claire-Helene. *Miro: Earth and Sky*. New York: Chelsea House, 1993.

Blyth, Beatrice. "Northern Paiute Bands in Oregon." *American Anthropologist* 40 (1938): 402.

Boas, Franz. *Primitive Art*. New York: Dover Publications, 1955.

Bower, Bruce. "Visions on the Rocks." *Science News* 150 (1996): 216.

Boyd, Robert. *Wandering Wagons: Meek's Lost Emigrants of 1845*. Bend: The High Desert Museum, 1993.

Brandt, John. "Pictographs and Petroglyphs of the Southwest Indians." In *Astronomy of the Ancients*. Ed. Kenneth Brecher. Cambridge: MIT Press, 1980.

But, P., et al. "Rediscovery and Reproductive Biology of *Pleuropogon oregonus*." *Madrono* 32, no. 3 (1984): 189.

Carlson, Roy. "Klamath Henwas and Other Stone Sculpture." *American Anthropologist* 61 (1959): 88-96.

Clark, Ella. *Indian Legends of the Pacific Northwest*. Berkeley: University of California, 1953.

Cope, E.D. "The Silver Lake of Oregon and Its Region." *The American Naturalist* (November 1889): 970.

Copper, Forest. *Introducing Doctor Daly*. Lake County Historical Society. Bend: Maverick Publications, 1986.

Couch, Richard, and Stephen Johnson. "The Warner Valley Earthquake Sequence of May and June 1968." *The Ore Bin* 30 (1968): 191.

Cressman, L.S. *Early Man in Oregon*. Eugene: University of Oregon, 1940.

_____. *Petroglyphs of Oregon*. Eugene: University of Oregon, 1937.

_____. *The Sandal and the Cave*. Corvallis: Oregon State University Press, 1981.

Crook, George. *General George Crook: His Autobiography*. Norman: University of Oklahoma Press, 1960.

Csuti, Blair, et al. *Atlas of Oregon Wildlife*. Corvallis: Oregon State University Press, 1997.

Cunkle, James, and Markus Jacquemain. *Stone Magic of the Ancients*. Phoenix: Golden West Publishers, 1996.

Curtin, Jeremiah. *Myths of the Modocs*. Boston: Little, Brown and Co., 1912.

Davis, George. *Scott-Applegate Trail Atlas and Gazetteer 1846-1847*. Soap Creek Enterprises, 1995.

Davis, W.N. *Sagebrush Corner: The Opening of California's Northeast*. New York: Garland Publishing. 1974.

Devereux, Paul. *Shamanism and the Mystery Lines*. St. Paul: Llewellyn Publishers, 1994.

Douglass, W.A. *Basque Sheepherders of the American West*. Reno: University of Nevada Press, 1985.

Eastman, D.C. *Rare and Endangered Plants of Oregon*. Beautiful America Publishing, 1990.

Elder, Diane. "Way Back When." *Lake County*. Lake County Historical Society, 1983: 1.

Eliade, Mircea. *The Sacred and the Profane: The Nature of Religion*. Orlando: Harcourt Brace Jovanovich, Publishers, 1959.

_____. *Shamanism: Archaic Techniques of Ecstasy*. Princeton University Press, 1964.

Emerson, William. *The Applegate Trail of 1846*. Ashland: Ember Enterprises, 1996.

Estergreen, Morgan. *Kit Carson*. Norman: University of Oklahoma Press, 1962.

Ewing, Eve. "Summer Solstice: New Discoveries from San Carlos Mesa." *Rock Art Papers* 7 (1990): 23.

Ferguson, Denzel, and Nancy Ferguson. *Oregon's Great Basin Country*. Burns: Gail Graphics, 1978.

Fiero, Bill. *Geology of the Great Basin*. Reno: University of Nevada Press, 1986.

Fitch, Robert. *Silver Lake: The Way It Was*. Eugene: Western Printers, 1991.

Fowler, Catherine, and Sven Liljeblad. "Northern Paiute." In *Handbook of North American Indians*, vol. 11. Washington, D.C.: Smithsonian, 1986.

Fox, Oliver. *Astral Projection*. New York: Carol Publishing, 1993.

Franklin, Jerry, and C.T. Dyrness. *Natural Vegetation of Oregon and Washington*. Corvallis: Oregon State University Press, 1973.

Frazer, Sir James. *The Illustrated Golden Bough: A Study in Magic and Religion*. New York: Simon and Schuster, 1996.

_____. *The Worship of Nature*. London: Macmillan, 1926.

Fremont, John C. *Exploring Expedition to the Rocky Mountains*. Smithsonian Institution, 1988.

French, Giles. *Cattle Country of Pete French*. Portland: Binfords and Mort, 1965.

Garth, Thomas. "Atsugewi Ethnography." *Anthropological Record*. Berkeley: University of California Press, 1953: 129.

Gillis, Julia. *So Far From Home*. Oregon Historical Society Press, 1993.

Glassley, Ray. *Pacific Northwest Indian Wars*. Portland: Binfords and Mort, 1953.

Gooch, Sara, ed. *The Journal of the Modoc County Historical Society: Native American Issue* (1990).

_____. *The Journal of the Modoc County Historical Society: Warner Mountains Issue* (1991).

Gray, Edward. *William "Bill" W. Brown 1855-1941: Legend of Oregon's High Desert*. Salem: Your Town Press Inc., 1993.

Grayson, Donald. *The Desert's Past: A Natural Prehistory of the Great Basin*. Washington, D.C.: Smithsonian Institution, 1993.

Guard, Jennifer. *Wetland Plants of Oregon and Washington*. Vancouver: Lone Pine Publishing, 1995.

Gulick, Bill. *Roadside History of Oregon*. Missoula: Mountain Press Publishing Co., 1991.

Guse, Ernst-Gerhard. *Paul Klee: Dialogue with Nature*. Munich: Prestel-Verlag, 1991.

Hatton, Raymond. *Pioneer Homesteads of the Fort Rock Valley*. Portland: Binfords and Mort, 1982.

Heizer, Robert. "Sacred Rain Rocks of Northern California." *Papers on California Archaeology*: 33.

_____. "Some Prehistoric Bullroarers from California Caves." *University of California Archaeological Survey* (1960): 5.

Heizer, Robert, and Martin Baumhoff. *Prehistoric Rock Art of Nevada and Eastern California*. Berkeley: University of California Press, 1962.

Heizer, Robert, and Albert Elsasser. *The Natural World of the California Indians*. Berkeley: University of California Press, 1980.

Hill, James. *Some Mining Districts in Northeastern California and Northwestern Nevada*. Washington, D.C.: U.S. Government Printing Office, 1915.

Hill, Ray, and Beth Hill. *Indian Petroglyphs of the Pacific Northwest*. Saanichton: Hancock House, 1974.

Hopkins, Sarah Winnemucca. *Life Among the Paiutes*. Bishop: Sierra Media Inc., 1969.

Howe, Carrol. *Ancient Tribes of the Klamath Country*. Portland: Binfords and Mort, 1968.

Hult, Ruby. *Lost Mines and Treasures of the Pacific Northwest*. Portland: Binfords and Mort, 1957.

Jackman, E.R., and R.A. Long. *The Oregon Desert*. Caldwell: Caxton Printers, 1992.

Jackson, Philip, and Jon Kimerling. *Atlas of the Pacific Northwest*. Corvallis: Oregon State University Press, 1993.

Johnson, D.M., et al. *Atlas of Oregon Lakes*. Corvallis: Oregon State University Press, 1985.

Jones, Bernard. "Preliminary Investigation into a Southern California Summer Solstice Site." *Rock Art Papers* 3 (1986): 157.

_____. "The Sun Arrives at His Home." *Rock Art Papers* 6 (1989): 75.

Kaysing, Bill. *Great Hotsprings of the West*. Santa Barbara: Capra Press, 1990.

Kelly, Isabel. "Ethnography of the Surprise Valley Paiute." In *University of California Publications in American Archaeology and Ethnography*. Berkeley: University of California Press, 1932.

Keyser, James. *Indian Rock Art of the Columbia Plateau*. Seattle: University of Washington Press, 1992.

Kittredge, William. *Hole in the Sky*. New York: Alfred A. Knopf, 1992.

_____. *Owning It All*. Port Townsend: Graywolf Press, 1987.

_____. "Reimagining Warner." In *Heart of the Land*. New York: Pantheon Books, 1994.

_____. *We Are Not in This Together*. Port Townsend: Graywolf Press, 1984.

_____. *Who Owns the West?* San Francisco: Mercury House, 1996.

Kniffen, Fred. *Achomawi Geography*. Berkeley: University of California Press, 1927.

Kresek, Ray. *Fire Lookouts of Oregon and Washington*. Spokane: Historic Lookout Project, 1985.

Lange, Erwin. "A Collection of Articles on Meteorites." *The Ore Bin* 27, no. 2 (1968): 6.

Langbein, W.B. "Salinity and Hydrology of Closed Lakes." *Geological Survey Professional Paper 412*. Washington, D.C.: U.S. Government Printing Office, 1961.

Lanner, Ronald. *Trees of the Great Basin*. Reno: University of Nevada Press, 1984.

Larson, Charlie, and Jo Larson. *Central Oregon Caves*. Vancouver: ABC Publishing, 1987.

Lichtman, Jim. *The Lone Ranger's Code of the West*. Palm Desert: Scribbler's Ink Press, 1996.

Loring, Malcolm, and Louise Loring. *Pictographs and Petroglyphs of the Oregon Country*. Los Angeles: UCLA Institute of Archaeology, 1996.

Lucas, David. "Aspens." *Orion* (Spring 1997): 59.

Maclean, Norman. *A River Runs Through It*. Chicago: University of Chicago Press, 1976.

Mallery, Garick. "Pictographs of the North American Indians." In *Fourth Annual Report of the Bureau of Ethnology*. Washington, D.C.: U.S. Government Printing Office, 1886.

_____. "Picture Writing of the American Indian." In *Tenth Annual Report of the Bureau of Ethnology*. Washington, D.C.: U.S. Government Printing Office, 1893.

McArthur, Lewis. *Oregon Geographic Names*. Corvallis: Oregon State University Press, 1992.

McChristian, Douglas. *The U.S. Army in the West, 1870-1880*. Norman: University of Oklahoma Press, 1995.

McCune, Bruce, and Linda Geiser. *Macrolichens of the Pacific Northwest*. Corvallis: Oregon State University Press, 1997.

McGuire, Kelly, and Brian Hatoff. "A Prehistoric Bighorn Sheep Drive Complex." *Journal of California and Great Basin Anthropology* (1991): 95.

McPhee, John. *Basin and Range*. New York: Farrar, Straus, Giroux, 1981.

Merriam, Hart. *AN-NIK-A-DEL: The History of the Universe as Told by the Modesse Indians of California*. Boston: The Stratford Co., 1928.

Mihalyo, Daniel. *Wood Burners*. New York: Princeton Architectural Press, 1997.

Mikesh, Robert C. "Japan's World War II Balloon Bomb Attacks on North America." In *Smithsonian Annals of Flight*, no. 9. Washington, D.C.: Smithsonian Press, 1972.

Minor, Rick, et al. *Cultural Resource Overview of the BLM Lakeview District, South-Central Oregon: Archaeology, Ethnography, History*. Eugene: University of Oregon Anthropological Papers, no. 16 (1979).

Mitchell, James. *Gem Trails of Oregon*. Baldwin Park: Gem Guides Book Co., 1989.

Momnzingo, Hugh. *Shrubs of the Great Basin*. Reno: University of Nevada Press, 1987.

Myrick, David. *Railroads of Nevada and Eastern California*, vol. 1. Berkeley: Howell-North Books, 1962.

Nielsen, L.E., et al. *Pioneer Roads of Central Oregon*. Bend: Maverick Publications, 1985.

Norris, Kathleen. *Amazing Grace: A Vocabulary of Faith*. New York: Riverhead Books, 1998.

Oliphant, Orin. *On the Cattle Ranges of the Oregon Country*. Seattle: University of Washington Press, 1968.

Olmsted, D.L., and O.C. Stewart. "Achumawi." In *Handbook of North American Indians*, vol. 8. Washington, D.C.: Smithsonian, 1978.

Oregon Natural Heritage Program. *Rare, Threatened and Endangered Species of Oregon*. Portland: Oregon Natural Heritage Program, 1998.

Orr, Elizabeth, et al. *Geology of Oregon*. Dubuque: Kendall Hunt Publishing Co., 1992.

Palmer, Kevin. "California Imagery Comes to Alturas." *The Journal of the Modoc County Historical Society* (1989).

Patterson, Alex. *A Field Guide to the Rock Art Symbols of the Greater Southwest*. Boulder: Johnson Books, 1992.

Peers, Laura. "Trade and Change on the Columbia Plateau." *Columbia* (winter 1966): 7.

Pennak, Robert. *Fresh-Water Invertebrates of the United States*. New York: The Ronald Press Co., 1953.

Petersen, David. *Among the Aspen*. Northland Publishing Co., 1991.

Peterson, N.V. "Lake County's New Continuous Geyser." *The Ore Bin* 21, no. 9 (September 1959): 83-88.

_____. "Oregon Sunstones." *The Ore Bin* 32, no. 12 (December 1972): 197-241.

Peterson, N.V. and E.A. Groh. "Crack-In-The-Ground, Lake County, Oregon." *The Ore Bin* 26, no. 9 (September 1964): 158-166.

_____. "Maars of South-Central Oregon." *The Ore Bin* 25, no. 5 (May 1963): 73-88.

Pettigrew, Richard. *Archaeological Investigations on the East Shore of Lake Abert, Lake County, Oregon*. Eugene: University of Oregon Anthropological Papers, 1985.

Phillips, K.N., and A.S. Van Denburgh. "Hydrology and Geochemistry of Abert, Summer and Other Closed-Basin Lakes in South-Central Oregon." *Geological Survey Professional Paper 502-B*. Washington, D.C.: U.S. Government Printing Office, 1971.

Porter, Gladys. "The History of Willow Ranch." *The Journal of the Modoc County Historical Society* (1987): 101.

Prosek, James. *Trout*. New York: Alfred A. Knopf, 1996.

Pugh, Richard. "The Diamond Lake Fireball of March 28, 1994." *Oregon Geology* 57, no. 4 (July 1995): 93.

Quinn, Arthur. *Hell with the Fire Out: A History of the Modoc War*. Boston: Faber and Faber, Inc., 1997.

Ramsey, Jarold. *Coyote Was Going There: Indian Literature of the Oregon Country*. Seattle: University of Washington Press. 1977.

Rafter, John. "Searching for More Sun and Net Designs." *Rock Art Papers* 9 (1992): 135.

Ray, Vern. *Primitive Pragmatists: The Modoc Indians of Northern California*. Seattle: University of Washington Press, 1963.

Raymond, Anan. "Two Historic Aboriginal Game-Drive Enclosures in the Eastern Great Basin." *Journal of California and Great Basin Anthropology*. Banning: Malki Museum, 1982: 23.

Roach, Mary. "Ancient Altered States." *Discover* (June 1998).

Robin, Marc, and Eve Ewing. "The Sun Is In His House." *Rock Art Papers* 6 (1989): 29.

Ryser, Fred A., Jr. *Birds of the Great Basin*. Reno: University of Nevada Press, 1985.

Sammel, Edward, and Robert Craig. *The Geothermal Hydrology of Warner Valley*. Washington, D.C.: U.S. Government Printing Office, 1981.

Schaafsma, Polly. "Trance and Transformation in the Canyons: Shamanism and Early Art on the Colorado Plateau." In *Shamanism and Rock Art in North America*. San Antonio: Rock Art Foundation Inc., 1994.

Schiffman, Robert, ed. "Visions of the Sky." In *Archaeological and Ethnological Studies of California Indian Astronomy*. Salinas: Coyote Press, 1988.

Schwantes, Carlos. *Hard Traveling: A Portrait of Work Life in the New Northwest*. Lincoln: University of Nebraska Press, 1994.

_____. *Railroad Signatures of the Pacific Northwest*. Seattle: University of Washington Press, 1993.

Seaman, N.G. *Indian Relics of the Pacific Northwest*. Portland: Binfords and Mort, 1967.

Sehgal, Linda. "Climbing Jacob's Ladder: Symbolism of a Fantastic Journey Along the Milky Way." *Rock Art Paper* 6 (1989): 83.

Shapiro, Michael, and Peter Haassrick. *Frederic Remington: The Masterworks*. New York: Harry N. Abrams, 1988.

Shirk, David L. *The Cattle Drives of David Shirk*. Portland: Champoeg Press, 1956.

Sigler, William, and John Sigler. *Fishes of the Great Basin*. Reno: University of Nevada Press, 1987.

Slifer, Dennis, and Jane Duffield. *Kokapelli*. Santa Fe: Ancient City Press, 1994.

Soloman, Anne. "Rock Art in Southern Africa." *Scientific American*. (November 1996): 106.

Steber, Rick, and Jerry Gildermeister. *Where Rolls the Oregon*. Bear Wallow Publishing Co., 1985.

Stephenson, Georgie. *The Growth of Lake County Oregon*. Lakeview: Lake County Historical Society, 1994.

Stern, Jane, and Michael Stern. *Way Out West*. New York: Harper Collins, 1993.

Stewart, Omer. "The Northern Paiute Bands." *Anthropological Records*. Berkeley: University of California Press, 1939: 127-146.

Studendieck, James, et al. *North American Range Plants*. Lincoln: University of Nebraska Press, 1992.

Takaki, Ronald. *Journey to Gold Mountain: The Chinese in 19th-Century America*. New York: Chelsea House Publishers, 1994.

Taylor, R.J. *Sagebrush Country: A Wildflower Sanctuary*. Mountain Press Publishing Co., 1992.

Trimble, Stephen. *The Sagebrush Ocean: A Natural History of the Great Basin*. Reno: University of Nevada Press, 1989.

Turpin, Solveig, ed. *Shamanism and Rock Art in North America*. San Antonio: Rock Art Foundation, 1994.

United States Fish and Wildlife Service. *Draft Recovery Plan for the Threatened and Rare Native Fishes of the Warner Basin and Alkali Subbasin*. Portland: United States Fish and Wildlife Service, 1997.

Van Wormer, Joe. *The World of the Pronghorn*. New York: Lippincott Co., 1969.

Verdi, Richard. *Klee and Nature*. New York: Rizzoli, 1984.

Walker, George, and Edward McHugh. *Mineral Resources of the Lost Forest Instant Wilderness Study Area, Oregon*. Washington, D.C.: Geological Survey, 1980.

Waters, Aaron. "A Structural and Petrographic Study of the Glass Buttes, Lake County Oregon." *Journal Geology* 35 (1927): 441-52.

Webber, Bert. *The Oregon and Applegate Trail Diary of Welborn Beeson in 1853*. Medford: Webb Research Group, 1993.

Wheat, Margaret. *Survival Arts of the Primitive Paiutes*. Reno: University of Nevada Press, 1967.

Whiting, Beatrice. *Paiute Sorcery*. New York: Viking Fund Publications in Anthropology, 1950.

Whitley, David. *A Guide to Rock Art Sites: Southern California and Southern Nevada*. Missoula: Mountain Press, 1996.

Williamson, Ray. *Living the Sky: The Cosmos of the American Indian*. Norman: University of Oklahoma Press, 1984.

Wormser, Richard. *Growing Up in the Great Depression*. New York: Atheneum, 1994.

_____. *Hoboes: Wandering in America*. New York: Walker and Co., 1994.

Yskavitch, James. *Oregon Wildlife Viewing Guide*. Helena: Falcon Press Publishing Co., 1994.

About the Author

MELVIN R. ADAMS was born and raised in the small town of Lakeview in the desert of eastern Oregon. His childhood revolved around the outdoors: hunting, fishing, camping, and backpacking. While earning a bachelor's degree in general science at Oregon State University, he returned to eastern Oregon each summer to survey roads in the Fremont National Forest. His experiences in the desert instilled in him a love for and deep interest in the natural and human history of the region.

After earning a master's degree with dual majors in biology and geology from the University of North Dakota, Adams began a career as a science teacher, first in Oregon then in California. He later returned to college to study environmental engineering, prompted in part by his growing concern for the environment of the West; afterward, he took a position as an engineer at the Hanford Nuclear Reservation in the Washington desert. For the past twenty-one years, his scientific expertise has focused on the environmental problems associated with nuclear waste disposal in arid environments. He is currently a senior scientist with CH2M Hill Hanford Group, Inc.

Adams has authored or co-authored many scientific and technical articles and papers, holds a patent related to isolation barriers for nuclear waste disposal, and is a published poet. In addition to exploring for undocumented petroglyph sites, his hobbies include nature photography, bird watching, and fly fishing. He lives in Richland, Washington, with his wife Onnie, a piano teacher. They have two grown daughters, Carrie and Heather.